ADVENTURE ROADS NORTH

The Story of
the Alaska Highway
and Other Roads in
The MILEPOST®

Volume 10, Number 1, 1983
Alaska Geographic®

The Alaska Geographic Society

To teach many more to better know and use our natural resources

Chief Editor: Robert A. Henning
Assistant Chief Editor: Barbara Olds
Editor: Kris Valencia
Photography Editor: Dianne Hofbeck
Editorial Assistant: Margy Kotick
Design: Sandra Harner
Maps: Jon.Hersh and David Shott

ALASKA GEOGRAPHIC®, ISSN 0361-1353, is published quarterly by The Alaska Geographic Society, Anchorage, Alaska 99509. Second-class postage paid in Edmonds, Washington 98020. Printed in U.S.A.

THE ALASKA GEOGRAPHIC SOCIETY is a nonprofit organization exploring new frontiers of knowledge across the lands of the polar rim, learning how other men and other countries live in their Norths, putting the geography book back in the classroom, exploring new methods of teaching and learning — sharing in the excitement of discovery in man's wonderful new world north of 51°16'.

MEMBERS OF THE SOCIETY RECEIVE *Alaska Geographic*®, a quality magazine which devotes each quarterly issue to monographic in-depth coverage of a northern geographic region or resource-oriented subject.

MEMBERSHIP DUES in The Alaska Geographic Society are $30 per year: $34 to non-U.S. addresses, U.S. funds. (Eighty percent of each year's dues is for a one-year subscription to *Alaska Geographic*®.) Order from The Alaska Geographic Society, Box 4-EEE, Anchorage, Alaska 99509; (907) 274-0521.

MATERIAL SOUGHT: The editors of *Alaska Geographic*® seek a wide variety of informative material on the lands north of 51°16' on geographic subjects — anything to do with resources and their uses (with heavy emphasis on quality color photography) — from Alaska, Northern Canada, Siberia, Japan — all geographic areas that have a relationship to Alaska in a physical or economic sense. We do not want material done in excessive scientific terminology. A query to the editors is suggested. Payments are made for all material upon publication.

CHANGE OF ADDRESS: The post office does not automatically forward *Alaska Geographic*® when you move. To insure continuous service, notify us six weeks before moving. Send us your new address and zip code (and moving date), your old address and zip code, and if possible send a mailing label from a copy of *Alaska Geographic*®. Send this information to *Alaska Geographic*® Mailing Offices, 130 Second Avenue South, Edmonds, Washington 98020.

MAILING LISTS: We have begun making our members' names and addresses available to carefully screened publications and companies whose products and activities might be of interest to you. If you would prefer not to receive such mailings, please so advise us, and include your mailing label (or your name and address if label is not available).

Library of Congress cataloging in publication data:
Main entry under title:

Adventure roads north.

(Alaska geographic, ISSN 0361-1353;v. 10, no. 1)
1. Roads—Alaska. I. Milepost. II. Series.
F901.A266 vol. 10, no. 1   917.98s   82-22656
[HE356.A4]   [917.98]
ISBN 0-88240-171-8

Cover — *View of 13,832-foot Mount Hayes from the Denali Highway, 97 miles east of Cantwell. The highest peaks of the Alaska Range are visible — weather permitting — from the Denali.* (Jon R. Nickles)

Previous page — *A clear evening on the Taylor Highway near the summit of Mount Fairplay at Milepost 33. Milepost markers are simple steel rods with a mileage flag at the top.* (Sharon Paul, staff)

STATEMENT OF OWNERSHIP MANAGEMENT and CIRCULATION

(Required by 39 U.S.C. 3685)

Alaska Geographic® is a quarterly publication, home offices, Box 4-EEE, Anchorage, Alaska 99509. Editor is Robert A. Henning. Publisher is The Alaska Geographic Society, Box 4-EEE, Anchorage, Alaska 99509. Owners are Robert A. Henning and Phyllis G. Henning, Box 4-EEE, Anchorage, Alaska 99509. Robert A. Henning and Phyllis G. Henning, husband and wife, are owners of 100 percent of all common stock outstanding.

Alaska Geographic® has a paid circulation of 16,915 subscribers and newsstand buyers.

I certify that statements above are correct and complete:
ROBERT A. HENNING
Editor

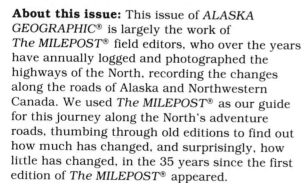

Clockwise from left — MILEPOST *field editor Sharon Paul's camper, and husband Norman Nault, parked outside the Manley Roadhouse.* (Sharon Paul, staff)

The Alaska state ferry Tustumena loads passengers and vehicles at Seward. (Tom Walker)

Eric Muelling and Barbara Sheer, with canoe, try their luck hitchhiking out of Tok. (Sharon Paul, staff)

On Alaska roads, moose have the right-of-way. These unpredictable animals have been known to challenge unyielding motorists. (Tom Walker)

Look for — and listen for — Canada geese in Alaska, especially in the fall. (Kenneth Naversen)

A rainy night on the Glenn Highway just outside of Tok. (Sharon Paul, staff)

About this issue: This issue of *ALASKA GEOGRAPHIC®* is largely the work of *The MILEPOST®* field editors, who over the years have annually logged and photographed the highways of the North, recording the changes along the roads of Alaska and Northwestern Canada. We used *The MILEPOST®* as our guide for this journey along the North's adventure roads, thumbing through old editions to find out how much has changed, and surprisingly, how little has changed, in the 35 years since the first edition of *The MILEPOST®* appeared.

We thank the many fine photographers who have contributed their work. Our thanks also to Terrence Cole, for his editorial contribution and review of the text.

In putting together this issue, we used as reference the records of the Bureau of Public Roads, Public Roads Administration, the Alaska Road Commission, and other historical documents administered by the National Archives of the United States, including Theodore A. Huntley's report on the construction of the Alaska Highway in 1942; *Fifty Years of Highways*, the Alaska Department of Public Works, Division of Highways; and various books from Alaska Northwest Publishing Company's North Country library.

TABLE OF CONTENTS

Opposite — *Denali National Park road winds across tundra-covered hills toward 20,320-foot Mount McKinley. The 90-mile gravel road is the only road in the park.* (Sharon Paul, staff)

Above - *Dall sheep browse for food along the road in Denali National Park. These wild, white sheep are found in all major mountain ranges in Alaska. In summer, look for them high up on rocky mountainsides.* (Jon R. Nickles)

INTRODUCTION

The roads of the north . . . the trails of only a few yesterday years in history . . . are perhaps the most important elements in understanding the geographic-economic history of Alaska and neighboring lands of Northwest Canada.

Roads have come slowly to the North, and it was the crash building of the Alaska Highway during World War II, that accelerated a lot of other wilderness road projects that today make up a fascinating matrix of roads . . . many going off into The Bush, seemingly nowhere . . . some connecting tiny settlements of seeming inconsequence as far as cities go . . . most gravel, a few blacktop . . . but all reaching farther and farther into the wilderness . . . changing the land in the immediate vicinity of milepost markers, but still barely making a mark in the vastness of poplar and spruce and birch and cottonwood rolling across the sweeping tundra and rolling hills, disappearing in the clefted valleys of the great ranges.

Here and there in the scattered villages back of and beyond the occasional more city-like settlements there are new log cabins in the old tradition, new pre-fabs of the new generation, small new clearings that mark both the coming of new men, and their passing.

The game is sometimes on and near the roads, favoring the early and late hours of the day . . . bear, moose, caribou, sheep, goats, the smaller creatures of shore and stream, the feathered creatures and the fish that have known no artificial origins . . . but late rising man who mostly sits, driving content through all this land, seldom sees or enjoys these things. Pity him for he knows not and he misses much.

But for others, the air is wine and the views are endless . . . the natural land, the people, and the unknown, unseen, around the next bend, over the next hill, beckon on and on. It is a land that promises much for those who see horizons . . .

And that is where the Adventure Roads of the North lead you . . . on and on into infinite horizons. It is for you this book has been built . . . to promise good things to come for those who have not yet driven north . . . to bring back cherished memories for those who have.

Sincerely,

Robert A. Henning, President
The Alaska Geographic Society

P.S. Get a copy of *The MILEPOST*® for up-to-the-minute detail, maps, etc. ($11.95 plus $1 fourth class or $3 first class from Alaska Northwest Publishing Company, Box 4-EEE, Anchorage, Alaska 99509). And take note of the up-front admonition to drive at moderate pace on all back country gravel . . . it's considerate for your motorist friends you meet going the other direction . . . it saves blowouts from hot friction buildup . . . and it makes it easier to slow down, pull off the road and drink in the smell, the taste, and the always changing vista.

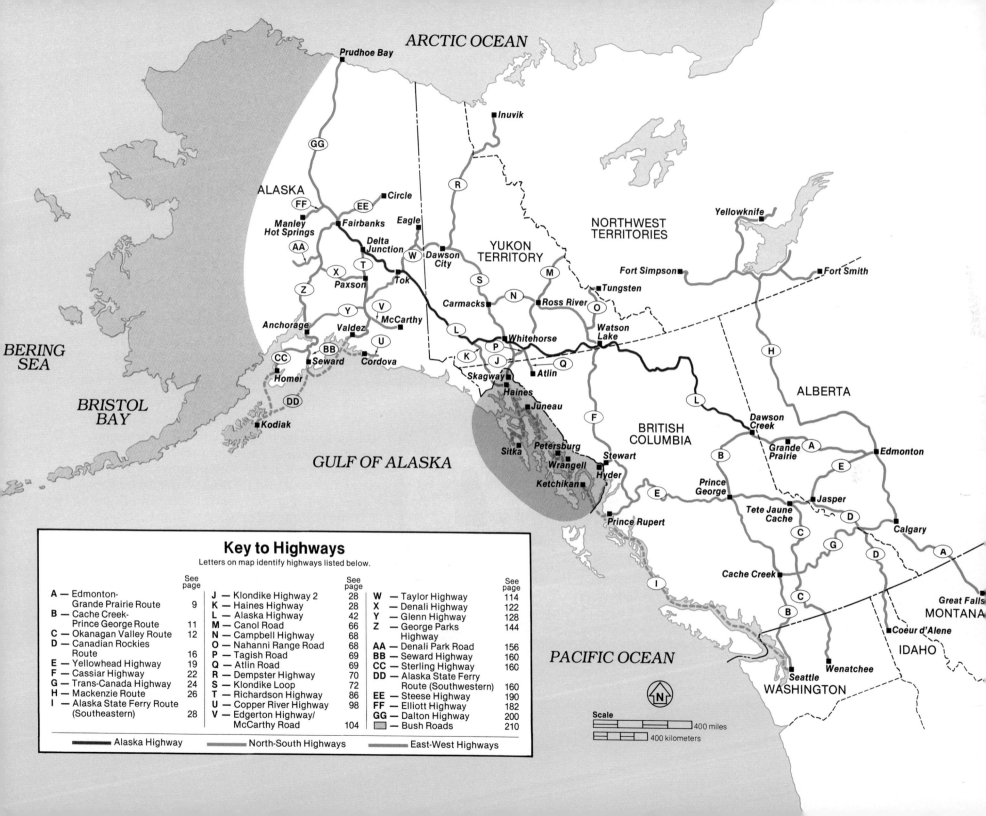

ARCTIC OCEAN

Prudhoe Bay

ALASKA

Circle

GG

FF

Manley Hot Springs

EE

Fairbanks

Eagle

Delta Junction

AA

X

T

Paxson

Tok

W

Dawson City

YUKON TERRITORY

Z

Y

V

McCarthy

Anchorage

Valdez

U

S

Carmacks

N

Ross River

M

O

Watson Lake

Fort Simpson

NORTHWEST TERRITORIES

Yellowknife

Fort Smith

Tungsten

L

Whitehorse

BB

CC

Seward

Cordova

P

Homer

DD

K

J

Q

Atlin

Skagway

Kodiak

Haines

Juneau

F

H

Dawson Creek

ALBERTA

BERING SEA

BRISTOL BAY

GULF OF ALASKA

Sitka

Petersburg

Wrangell

Ketchikan

Stewart

Hyder

BRITISH COLUMBIA

L

A

Grande Prairie

B

E

Edmonton

Prince Rupert

E

Prince George

E

Tete Jaune Cache

Jasper

D

C

G

Calgary

Cache Creek

C

D

A

I

B

Great Falls

MONTANA

PACIFIC OCEAN

Seattle

Wenatchee

Coeur d'Alene

IDAHO

WASHINGTON

Key to Highways

Letters on map identify highways listed below.

	See page			See page			See page
A — Edmonton-Grande Prairie Route	9	J — Klondike Highway 2	28	W — Taylor Highway	114
B — Cache Creek-Prince George Route	11	K — Haines Highway	28	X — Denali Highway	122
C — Okanagan Valley Route	12	L — Alaska Highway	42	Y — Glenn Highway	128
D — Canadian Rockies Route	16	M — Canol Road	66	Z — George Parks Highway	144
E — Yellowhead Highway	19	N — Campbell Highway	68	AA — Denali Park Road	156
F — Cassiar Highway	22	O — Nahanni Range Road	68	BB — Seward Highway	160
G — Trans-Canada Highway	24	P — Tagish Road	69	CC — Sterling Highway	160
H — Mackenzie Route	26	Q — Atlin Road	69	DD — Alaska State Ferry Route (Southwestern)	160
I — Alaska State Ferry Route (Southeastern)	28	R — Dempster Highway	70	EE — Steese Highway	190
		S — Klondike Loop	72	FF — Elliott Highway	182
		T — Richardson Highway	86	GG — Dalton Highway	200
		U — Copper River Highway	98	▨ — Bush Roads	210
		V — Edgerton Highway/McCarthy Road	104		

▬▬▬ Alaska Highway   ▬▬▬ North-South Highways   ▬▬▬ East-West Highways

N

Scale

400 miles

400 kilometers

ACROSS CANADA

The southern access routes to the Alaska Highway

Rich soil of central and western Alberta yields wheat and other grain crops, and supports an important livestock industry. (Joseph Allen Hofbeck, reprinted from *The MILEPOST®*)

The Alaska Highway begins at Dawson Creek, British Columbia, some 500 miles due north of the United States-Canada border. In the early years of the Alaska Highway, many travelers found just getting to the start of the highway a challenge. Celia Hunter, who came up the Alcan in 1951, drove to Dawson Creek via Edmonton, Slave Lake, and High Prairie, the only access route to the Alaska Highway back then, and a long one.

Idaho residents Howard and Sara Paul headed for the Alaska Highway in 1957 with a Cadillac, trailer, three extra tires, and four extra tire tubes. They drove to Dawson Creek by way of Prince George and the Hart Highway, then a dirt and gravel road. "From Prince George to Dawson Creek," they recalled, "it was raining so bad that we took all day to drive 50 miles."

Today, a network of highways across

Alberta and British Columbia, and up into Northwest Territories, offers a variety of routes for Alaska-bound travelers. The roads (with few exceptions) are now all paved, primary highways. These south-north and east-west access routes are described in the following pages.

Edmonton-Grande Prairie Route

Prior to 1952, this travel route from Great Falls, Montana, north through Edmonton and Grande Prairie, Alberta, to Dawson Creek, British Columbia, was the only way to reach the Alaska Highway by automobile from the Lower 48.

The 867-mile route from Great Falls to Dawson Creek cuts through the fertile wheat lands of central Alberta and passes through the province's two largest cities: the flat, sprawling business centre of Calgary; and

Scale
200 miles
200 kilometers

Right — *North Saskatchewan River reflects the modern skyline of Edmonton, Alberta's capital and largest city.* (F. Grant, Canadian Government Office of Tourism; reprinted from *The MILEPOST®*)

Below — *Long, straight section of highway near Grande Prairie, a centre for agriculture, forestry, and petroleum industry in northern Alberta. Here, motorists are only 79 miles from Dawson Creek, British Columbia, the start of the Alaska Highway.* (Patrick Hawkes, staff)

Edmonton, the capital of Alberta, with a population of half-a-million people.

From Edmonton, the route swings northwest on Highway 43 to Valleyview, then west on Highway 34 to Grande Prairie and Highway 2 across the border to Dawson Creek, Milepost 0 of the Alaska Highway. Prior to the completion of Highway 43 in October of 1955, motorists bound for the Alaska Highway had to drive north from Edmonton, negotiating treacherous dirt roads around Lesser Slave Lake described in the 1950 edition of *The MILEPOST®* as "exceedingly muddy in wet weather, at times almost impassable." New roads — such as Highway 43 — and paving of old roads has shortened and improved this access route to the Alaska Highway. Today, all roads to Dawson Creek are paved, primary routes.

Cache Creek-
Prince George Route

This major west access route to the Alaska Highway links west coast travelers with Dawson Creek by going up through the middle of British Columbia.

Beginning at Seattle, Washington, this route heads north through British Columbia's rugged Fraser River Canyon to Cache Creek and Highway 97. Sometimes called the Cariboo Highway, after the old Cariboo wagon road used by gold seekers and settlers during British Columbia's pioneer days, Highway 97 leads through

Above — *Barkerville Provincial Historic Park, a reconstructed and restored Cariboo gold rush town, is 55 miles east of Quesnel. Stagecoaches once connected Barkerville to other communities on the Cariboo wagon road.* (Staff)

Right — *A tributary of the Fraser River, the Thompson River has two main branches. Pictured here is the South Thompson River, which flows beside the highway for some 40 miles south of Cache Creek.* (Ray T. Weisgerber)

View of Upper Pine River from the Hart Highway, about 100 miles southwest of Dawson Creek. The John Hart-Peace River Highway, a continuation of Highway 97, provided a more direct route to the Alaska Highway from the west when it opened in 1952. (Staff)

ranch and lake country to Prince George, third biggest city in the province.

From Prince George, the 252-mile John Hart Highway leads northeast to Dawson Creek. The Hart Highway opened in 1952, providing a more direct access route to the Alaska Highway from the Pacific Coast highway system by eliminating the long drive east to Edmonton for motorists from the west coast. From Seattle to Milepost 0 of the Alaska Highway, it is approximately 815 miles via this route.

Okanagan Valley Route

From eastern Washington's Okanogan Valley to Canada's Okanagan Valley (where the "o" becomes an "a"), Highway 97 leads past lush orchards and rolling grasslands to Kamloops and the start of Yellowhead Highway 5. Completed in 1969, Yellowhead Highway 5 provided a new route for Alaska Highway-bound motorists. (Prior to 1969, motorists continued west from Kamloops on Highway 97 to Prince George.)

The 211-mile Yellowhead Highway 5 follows the Thompson River's north fork past ordered farmlands and unspoiled wilderness to Tete Jaune Cache on Yellowhead Highway 16. From Tete Jaune Cache, the shortest route to Dawson Creek and the start of the Alaska Highway is west on Yellowhead Highway 16 to Prince George, then north on the Hart Highway (an added 420 miles). This access route — from Wenatchee, Washington, to Tete Jaune Cache, British Columbia — is 539 miles.

Above — *Small farm on outskirts of Little Fort, in the North Thompson river valley, about 155 miles south of Tete Jaune Cache on Yellowhead Highway 5.* (David Skidmore, reprinted from *The MILEPOST®*)

Right — *Blossom time in the Okanagan Valley is from mid-April to mid-May. Apples will be harvested from this orchard in the fall.* (Glen Forster)

Surrounded by rocky hills of sagebrush, cactus, and pine, irrigation unlocks the wealth of the dry Okanogan Valley.
(Mike Orvos)

Canadian Rockies Route

Since the completion of the Alaska Highway in 1942, new highways have branched out to connect the growing cities of western Canada, providing motorists with a choice of scenic routes to the North. One such combination of highways is the travel route from Idaho's panhandle up through Canada's Rocky Mountains to Jasper, Alberta. It is a 484-mile drive from Coeur d'Alene, Idaho, to Jasper via this route.

From northern Idaho, Highway 95 leads

Left — *View of Peyto Lake from Icefields Parkway overlook at Bow Summit. The play of light on the glacier-floured waters of the lake give it its intense color.* (Steve Owlett)

Above — *Bonners Ferry in Idaho's panhandle is approximately 31 miles south of Kingsgate, the U.S.-Canada border crossing.* (Blaine Schultz)

Right — *Terraced viewpoints around Athabasca Falls allow for closeup look at this magnificent waterfall. The falls are located just south of Jasper off the Icefields Parkway, seen in distance.* (Ray T. Weisgerber)

north across the Canadian border to Highway 93, a wide, paved highway that climbs northwest through the Canadian Rockies to the Icefields Parkway. The spectacular parkway winds north through the heart of the Rocky Mountains, past Columbia Icefield and Athabasca Glacier, to Jasper, townsite and headquarters of Jasper National Park. At Jasper, Alaska Highway-bound motorists may either turn east on the Yellowhead Highway to connect with the Edmonton-Grande Prairie route, or turn west on the Yellowhead for Prince George and the Hart Highway to Dawson Creek.

Above — *A not uncommon sight for motorists in the high Rockies: Rocky Mountain goats grazing alongside the road. Their feet acting as nonskid pads, these animals can be seen climbing to precipitous heights on surrounding mountain peaks.* (Staff)

Right — *Sunwapta Pass, elevation 6,675 feet, on the Icefields Parkway marks the boundary between Banff and Jasper national parks.* (Ray T. Weisgerber)

Yellowhead Highway

Yellowhead Highway 16 extends from Winnipeg, Manitoba, to Prince Rupert on the west coast of British Columbia. The 456-mile section of highway between Prince George and Prince Rupert was first covered in *The MILEPOST®* in 1963, the year Alaska inaugurated state ferry service from Prince Rupert to Southeastern Alaska. Construction of the 450-mile section of highway between Prince George and Edmonton was completed a few years later, creating a new northern transprovincial highway.

Today, the Yellowhead Highway from Edmonton to Prince Rupert is an important travel route for Alaska-bound motorists. The highway intersects all other north-south

Left — *Fort St. James, 37 miles north of Yellowhead Highway 16, was an isolated outpost of the Hudson's Bay Company in the late 1800s.* (Patrick Hawkes, staff)

Above — *Late afternoon sunlight casts shadows over a hayfield in the Bulkley River valley near Smithers. Peak in background is Hudson Bay Mountain.* (David Skidmore)

19

Opposite — *Massive Mount Robson, highest peak in the Canadian Rockies at 12,972 feet, can be seen from the Yellowhead Highway just west of Yellowhead Pass.* (Ray T. Weisgerber)

Left — *Prince Rupert, port of call for Alaska-bound ferries, marks the western end of Yellowhead Highway 16.* (Patrick Hawkes, staff)

Below — *Communal houses at 'Ksan, located just off the Yellowhead Highway near Hazelton. A replica Gitksan Indian village, 'Ksan is open to the public from May to October.* (David Skidmore)

access routes, and provides the only overland access to Prince Rupert, departure point for Alaska state ferries.

From Edmonton, Highway 16 leads west through Jasper National Park, cresting the Rockies at 3,760-foot Yellowhead Pass, named for a Hudson's Bay Company trapper and guide called *Tete Jaune* (yellow head) by French voyageurs.

After crossing the Rockies, the highway follows the great river valleys of northern British Columbia westward to the sea: the Fraser, Nechako, Bulkley, and Skeena. Nearing Prince Rupert, the Yellowhead enters the land of the Coast Indians, whose totems can be seen at Hazelton, 'Ksan, and Kitwanga.

21

Cassiar Highway

Some 300 miles west of Prince George, the Yellowhead Highway intersects one of British Columbia's newest roads, the Cassiar Highway. When it was completed in 1972, this 459-mile, mostly gravel, road connected the Yellowhead and Alaska highways, and opened up the rugged wilderness and magnificent scenery of northwestern British Columbia. The Cassiar Highway also provided first-time road access to Stewart, a small community at the head of Portland Canal, and to Hyder, Alaska, two miles west of Stewart.

The Cassiar Highway was originally an 87-mile side road from Milepost 649 on the Alaska Highway (just outside Watson Lake) to the Cassiar Asbestos Mine. Construction extended the road south to Stewart. From

Above — *The Cassiar Highway winds up the east side of the Coast Mountains of northwestern British Columbia. A few sections of the road have been paved, but most of the highway is still gravel-surfaced.* (Patrick Hawkes, staff)

Right — *St. Paul's Anglican Church at Kitwanga, at the south end of the Cassiar Highway, dates back to 1893 and is one of the finest examples of early wooden churches in the province.* (Steve Owlett)

Downtown Hyder, Alaska, is just 2.3 miles west of Stewart, British Columbia. Both of these small communities (Hyder's population is 90; Stewart's 1,500) are reached via a 40-mile side road from the Cassiar Highway. (Sharon Paul, staff)

Terrace, on the Yellowhead Highway, a logging road led north 95 miles to link up with the Watson Lake-Stewart Highway.

Today, the main southern approach of the Cassiar turns off the Yellowhead Highway 60 miles east of Terrace, crossing the Skeena River to the small Indian village of Kitwanga. About 100 miles north of Kitwanga, a 40-mile spur road leads west to Stewart and Hyder. North of the spur road turnoff, the Cassiar winds up the east side of the Coast Mountains to Dease Lake. Here, a rugged 74-mile road heads west to Telegraph Creek on the Stikine River. The Cassiar Highway ends at the Alaska Highway, 17 miles west of Watson Lake, Yukon Territory.

Primitive Telegraph Creek Road winds past the Indian village of Tahltan in the Stikine River canyon. The 74-mile-long Telegraph Creek Road leads west from Dease Lake to the community of Telegraph Creek, the former head of navigation on the Stikine River. (Rollo Pool, staff)

Sundown at beautiful Good Hope Lake. This lake, located about 60 miles south of the Alaska Highway, is just one of several pristine lakes along the Cassiar. (David Skidmore)

23

Trans-Canada Highway

Almost 5,000 miles long, Trans-Canada Highway 1 connects St. John's, Newfoundland, on Canada's Atlantic coast, with Victoria, British Columbia, on Vancouver Island off the Pacific coast. It is the world's longest national highway, and an important route for Alaska-bound motorists. The 650 miles of Trans-Canada Highway

Above — *Serene Lake Louise below Victoria Glacier is just off the Trans-Canada Highway, less than a two-hour drive west of Calgary.* (Ed and Katy Huston)

Right — *Described as a cross between a Scottish manor house and an 18th century French chateau, the Banff Springs Hotel is the grand old hotel of Banff National Park.* (David Skidmore)

between Calgary, Alberta, and Vancouver, British Columbia, connect with almost all of the access routes from the Lower 48 to Dawson Creek and the Alaska Highway.

West from Calgary, Trans-Canada Highway 1 crosses the Rocky Mountains through Banff and Yoho national parks. The highway also traverses Glacier National Park, where a wooden arch commemorates the September 1962 opening of the Trans-Canada Highway. From Cache Creek, the highway descends south and west along the Fraser River to the port of Vancouver.

Left — *Trans-Canada Highway 1 winds over the Rocky Mountains near Golden, paralleling the tracks of the Canadian Pacific Railway.* (Ray T. Weisgerber)

Below — *Vancouver, largest city in British Columbia and port of call for some Alaska-bound cruise ships, is on the Trans-Canada Highway.* (Blaine Schultz)

25

Mackenzie Route

The Mackenzie Highway is the gateway to the Northwest Territories highway system, a network of gravel roads linking the Far North settlements of Fort Simpson, Yellowknife, and Fort Smith. Milepost 0 of the Mackenzie is at Grimshaw, Alberta, in the Peace River country; the highway ends at Fort Simpson on the Mackenzie River in Northwest Territories.

The 590-mile Mackenzie Highway is also the longest of the five routes connecting communities around Great Slave Lake. The 212-mile highway to Yellowknife, second longest road, requires a ferry crossing at the

Above — *The Peace River flows east across northern Alberta. Explorer Alexander Mackenzie followed this great river in his quest for a route across the Rockies to the Pacific Ocean.* (Alberta Government photo, reprinted from *The MILEPOST®*)

Right — *Beached boat on Vale Island, near the Great Slave Lake community of Hay River.* (Ronne Heming)

Mackenzie River near Fort Providence. The highway to Fort Smith leads through Wood Buffalo National Park, second largest park in the world. Short highways connect Hay River, Pine Point, and Fort Resolution.

The Mackenzie Route was first covered in the 1973 edition of *The MILEPOST*® as a side trip for Alaska-bound motorists. Completion of the new Liard Highway will connect the Mackenzie Highway with the Alaska Highway at Fort Nelson.

Left — *Wood bison, a slightly larger and darker animal than the plains bison, are protected in 17,300-square-mile Wood Buffalo National Park near Fort Smith.*
(Ronne Heming, reprinted from *The MILEPOST*®)

Below — *Yellowknife, capital of Northwest Territories since 1967, is located on the north shore of Great Slave Lake.*
(Jim Whyard, reprinted from *The MILEPOST*®)

Right — *Alaska state ferry* Matanuska *loads vehicles at Seattle's Pier 48. The state ferries sail out of Seattle and Prince Rupert for Southeastern Alaska.* (Staff)

Below — *Seattle's waterfront was crowded with fortune hunters and the curious during the days of the Klondike gold rush. The mail steamer* Queen, *seen here, was loaded for Skagway, making the trip north in six days.* (Seattle Historical Society, reprinted from *The Skagway Story*)

SEA AND LAND ROUTES TO THE ALASKA HIGHWAY

Since the day the steamer *Portland* sailed into Seattle's Puget Sound in July of 1897, with news of the great Klondike gold strike, the Inside Passage has been the gateway to Alaska. This marine highway — almost 1,000 nautical miles long — extends from Seattle to Skagway, Alaska, a three-day voyage by ferry along the rugged coast of British Columbia and through the narrow waterways of Southeastern Alaska's Alexander Archipelago.

Alaska state ferry service to Southeastern Alaska was inaugurated in 1963, providing

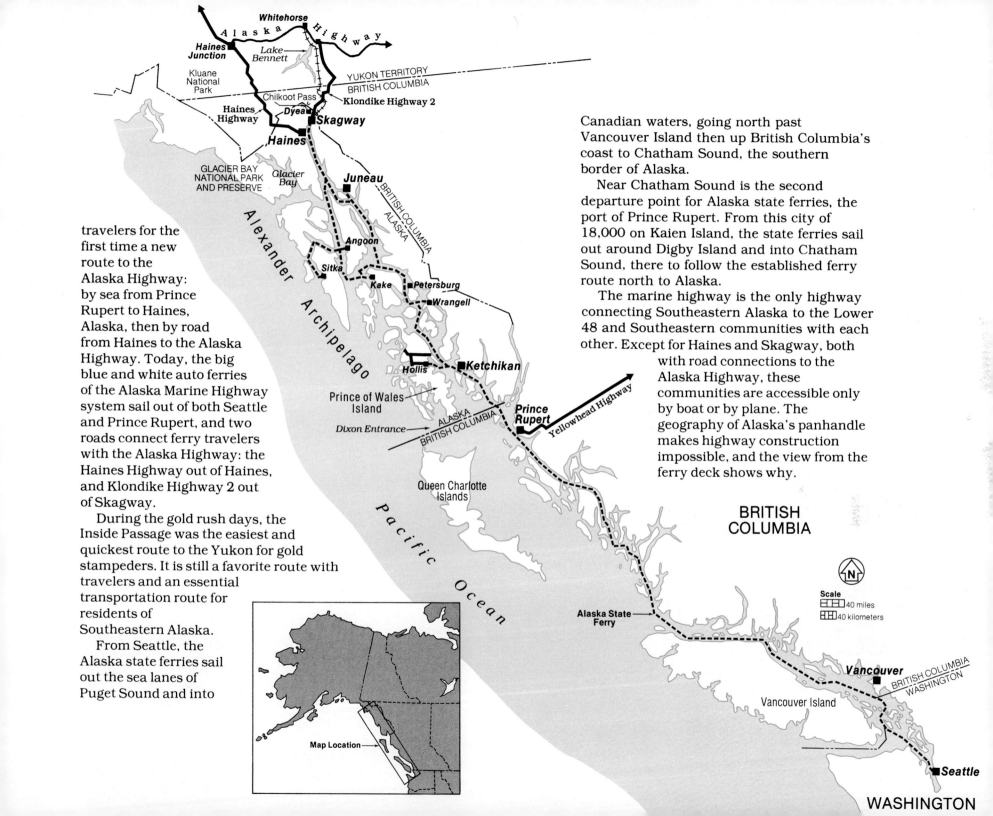

Whitehorse

A l a s k a   H i g h w a y

Haines Junction

Lake Bennett

Kluane National Park

YUKON TERRITORY
BRITISH COLUMBIA

Chilkoot Pass

Klondike Highway 2

Haines Highway

Dyea

Skagway

Haines

GLACIER BAY NATIONAL PARK AND PRESERVE

Glacier Bay

Juneau

BRITISH COLUMBIA
ALASKA

Angoon

Alexander Archipelago

Sitka

Kake

Petersburg

Wrangell

Hollis

Ketchikan

Prince of Wales Island

Dixon Entrance

ALASKA
BRITISH COLUMBIA

Prince Rupert

Yellowhead Highway

Queen Charlotte Islands

Pacific Ocean

BRITISH COLUMBIA

Scale
40 miles
40 kilometers

Alaska State Ferry

Vancouver

BRITISH COLUMBIA
WASHINGTON

Vancouver Island

Map Location

Seattle

WASHINGTON

travelers for the first time a new route to the Alaska Highway: by sea from Prince Rupert to Haines, Alaska, then by road from Haines to the Alaska Highway. Today, the big blue and white auto ferries of the Alaska Marine Highway system sail out of both Seattle and Prince Rupert, and two roads connect ferry travelers with the Alaska Highway: the Haines Highway out of Haines, and Klondike Highway 2 out of Skagway.

During the gold rush days, the Inside Passage was the easiest and quickest route to the Yukon for gold stampeders. It is still a favorite route with travelers and an essential transportation route for residents of Southeastern Alaska.

From Seattle, the Alaska state ferries sail out the sea lanes of Puget Sound and into

Canadian waters, going north past Vancouver Island then up British Columbia's coast to Chatham Sound, the southern border of Alaska.

Near Chatham Sound is the second departure point for Alaska state ferries, the port of Prince Rupert. From this city of 18,000 on Kaien Island, the state ferries sail out around Digby Island and into Chatham Sound, there to follow the established ferry route north to Alaska.

The marine highway is the only highway connecting Southeastern Alaska to the Lower 48 and Southeastern communities with each other. Except for Haines and Skagway, both with road connections to the Alaska Highway, these communities are accessible only by boat or by plane. The geography of Alaska's panhandle makes highway construction impossible, and the view from the ferry deck shows why.

Right — *Wake of the Alaska state ferry* Malaspina *trails back towards misty islands of British Columbia.* (Dianne Hofbeck)

Below — *Prince Rupert harbor from Mount Hays viewpoint behind the city. The Queen Charlotte Islands are almost 100 miles west of Prince Rupert, out of sight of most Inside Passage travelers.* (Patrick Hawkes, staff)

Opposite — *Homestead on quiet Silver Bay, a long finger of ocean southeast of Sitka. Sawmill Creek Road leads south from Sitka to Herring Cove at the mouth of Silver Bay; local boat tours cruise into the bay.* (Sharon Paul, staff)

Above — *Wrangell Narrows, one of many narrow waterways in Southeastern Alaska's Alexander Archipelago, is navigated by an Alaska state ferry on its way to Petersburg, a community of 3,000 people located at the northern end of the narrows.* (Rollo Pool, staff)

Below — *Petersburg waterfront of fish processing plants and fishing boats is usually busy with activity. This fishing port on Mitkof Island is the 19th U.S. port in terms of value of commercial fish landings.* (Rollo Pool, staff)

This is a region of thousands of densely forested islands, mountains that rise steeply from the sea and glaciers that spill over into valleys from the snow-capped coastal peaks. The communities along the mainline ferry route — Ketchikan, Wrangell, Petersburg, Juneau, and Sitka — lie nestled between high mountains and water's edge. Scattered among the islands of the archipelago are other Southeastern communities — Angoon, Kake, Tenakee — also served by state ferries.

Navigating through narrow channels, past spruce and hemlock-covered hills and miles of lonely beach, the bustling communities of Southeastern come as a surprise in this quiet land. All are waterfront towns, dependent on the sea and land for a living, and their attractions and industry are uniquely Southeastern: salmon fishing, salmon bakes, and salmon derbies; Russian dancers and onion-domed churches; seiners, gillnetters, and trollers; logging trucks, lumbermills, and log booms; and the age-old art of the peoples who preceded the white man here, the totems of the Tlingit Indians.

Left — *Skunk cabbage, a preferred food of bears, grows in swampy woods and bogs in Southeastern Alaska.* (Sharon Paul, staff)

Below — *A boatman guides logs toward a mill near Petersburg. The coastal rain forests of Southeastern provide the bulk of commercial timber in Alaska.* (Rollo Pool, staff)

Totem face at Saxman Totem Park south of Ketchikan. Saxman village was founded in 1894 by Tlingit Indians; the totem art of the Tlingits is seen throughout Southeastern Alaska. (Rollo Pool, staff)

Right — *A fish bake is part of the activities at Petersburg's Little Norway Festival, held in May.* (Rollo Pool, staff)

Below — *A gillnetter works the waters of Lynn Canal on the last day of the gillnet season. This rainy September day is the fisherman's last chance to gillnet for salmon until the season opens again.* (Nicholas Prebezac, staff)

A catch of king salmon on ice. Southeastern accounts for a large portion of Alaska's commercial salmon harvest. (Sharon Paul, staff)

33

Low clouds touch the rooftops of homes on Mount Juneau, a 3,576-foot mountain rising up behind the city. The colonial-style mansion seen here is the Governor's Mansion, built in 1912.
(David Skidmore)

Above — *State ferry* Taku *at the downtown ferry terminal at Juneau; a second ferry terminal is located 14 miles north of the city at Auke Bay.*
(Sharon Paul, staff)

Below — *Sightseers on shore give scale to the jagged face of Reid Glacier. The glacier is located in Reid Inlet at Glacier Bay National Park and Preserve.*
(Dianne Hofbeck, staff)

Above — *Glacier Bay excursion boat anchors at Reid Glacier to allow passengers a close-up look at an iceberg.*
(Nicholas Prebezac, staff)

Right — *Tour boat is dwarfed by Riggs Glacier in Muir Inlet. The Glacier Bay fjord complex has 13 active tidewater glaciers and is accessible by plane or boat; state ferries do not cruise into Glacier Bay.*
(Rollo Pool, staff)

Right — *Skagway's waterfront was the scene of frantic activity in 1897-1898, as thousands arrived here, bound for the Klondike gold fields.* (Asahel Curtis, reprinted from *Chilkoot Pass*)

Below — *Skagway, on the north end of Taiya Inlet on Lynn Canal, is the only Southeastern community besides Haines that is connected to the Alaska Highway. Port of call for state ferries and cruise ships, Skagway was the gateway to the Klondike for gold stampeders in 1897 and 1898.* (Sharon Paul, staff)

Many of Skagway's wooden buildings, dating from the gold rush years, are included in Klondike Gold Rush National Historical Park. (Nicholas Prebezac, staff)

36

Some of the early gold seekers who sailed these waters in the late 1800s found gold at or near Juneau and Sitka, but by 1897 most were bound for Skagway, the portal to the Klondike gold fields.

In 1898, at the height of the Klondike gold rush, thousands landed at Skagway and nearby Dyea. The tent city that sprang up on the shore of Lynn Canal had all the elements of a boom town: a muddy main street lined with saloons, gamblers, dance hall girls, and even an infamous con man — Soapy Smith. This was a stopping-off place for men bound for the Klondike. From Skagway, they made their way over Chilkoot Pass (now a national historical park) or over the White Pass trail. A narrow-gauge railroad, the White Pass & Yukon Route, replaced the trails in 1900 and continues to offer train service between Skagway and Whitehorse.

Loaded down with cookstoves, food, clothes, and a hundred other items, gold seekers climbed Chilkoot Pass on their way from Skagway to Lake Bennett and the Yukon River, water passage to the Klondike. The Chilkoot Trail is managed as a historic back-country trail today by the National Park Service. (Cantwell, reprinted from Chilkoot Pass)

On Chilkoot Pass

In 1978, the final section of a road connecting Skagway with the Alaska Highway was completed. Formerly known as the Skagway-Carcross Road, Klondike Highway 2 is 100 miles of gravel highway, open in summer only. This important access route meets the Alaska Highway a few miles south of Whitehorse. (North of Whitehorse, the Klondike Highway continues to Dawson City.) Narrow and winding, the highway climbs over 3,290-foot White Pass, paralleling both the old gold rush trail and the railroad to Whitehorse.

Thirteen nautical miles southwest of Skagway is the port of Haines, Milepost 0 of the Haines Highway. The 155-mile Haines Highway, a mostly gravel highway through the magnificent Kluane country, was built in 1942 as a trunk road for military supplies to the Alaska Highway. The 1949 edition of *The MILEPOST®* forecast the importance of this road for Alaska-bound travelers, stating "there is every reason to believe that this trunk road will in time become an important link between Alaska Highway points and coastwise shipping." The highway ends at Haines Junction on the Alaska Highway, 100 miles west of Whitehorse.

Above — *Construction of the White Pass & Yukon Route railroad, begun in May 1898, eventually stopped foot traffic over the Chilkoot Pass from Dyea, near Skagway. The railroad was completed to Carcross on Lake Bennett in 1900.* (E.A. Hegg, reprinted from *Chilkoot Pass*)

Right — *White Pass & Yukon Route railway parallels Klondike Highway 2 between Skagway and the Alaska Highway. The railway operates between Skagway and Whitehorse year-round; Klondike Highway 2 is closed in winter.* (Sharon Paul, staff)

Left — *Klondike Highway 2, just south of Carcross, approaches Montana Mountain. The highway, narrow and gravel-surfaced for most of its length, opened in 1978.* (Sharon Paul, staff)

Below — *Lone bald eagle photographed at Chilkat River flats on the Haines Highway. This eagle-viewing area is about 19 miles north of Haines; best viewing time is mid-October to January.* (David Skidmore)

Vehicles drive off the state ferry at Haines, one of the two northern panhandle ports linked to the Alaska Highway. (Sharon Paul, staff)

39

Moonrise over Dezadeash Lake, a beautiful 15-mile-long lake 30 miles south of Haines Junction on the Haines Highway. (Karen Donelson)

Right — *The Haines Highway winds down into Haines Junction on the Alaska Highway.* (Karen Donelson)

Opposite — *Highest summit on the Haines Highway is Chilkat Pass, elevation 3,493 feet, approximately 63 road miles north of Haines.* (Sharon Paul, staff)

THE ALASKA HIGHWAY

History of the Alcan

Construction of the 1,520-mile-long Alaska Highway, a winding ribbon of road through the great wilderness separating Alaska and southern Canada, began in March 1942 and was completed by October of that same year. Built in less than eight months, the history of the Alaska Highway — from inception through its evolvement as an important and permanent artery of travel — spans many years and involves thousands of personalities.

Approaching the Alaska border, the highway swings northwest of the snow-covered Saint Elias Mountains. Aerial surveys helped locate the route of the highway around mountainous sections in 1942. (Glen Forster)

Routing of the Alaska Highway was along an existing air route from Edmonton via Fort St. John, Fort Nelson, Watson Lake, Whitehorse, and Big Delta, to Fairbanks. Ready access to the highway's southern terminus from the Lower 48 was also an important consideration: A straight line drawn from Fairbanks through Fort St. John connects with the industrial center of Chicago. Fort St. John was supply center for the pioneer road project. Whitehorse was headquarters of the Northwest Service Command and was also one of the largest construction camps on the highway.

Above — *Speed of construction was the overriding consideration in building the Alaska Highway, and the road initially was not noted for its carefully engineered grades and curves. Crews worked round-the-clock in the summer of 1942, often building three to four miles of road a day.* (Courtesy of U.S. Army, reprinted from *ALASKA®* magazine)

Left — *Spring breakup in the North turned some sections of the Alaska Highway into a quagmire in 1942. Engineers removed muskeg and topsoil then backfilled with gravel and rock, which promptly sank into the mud when the roadbed thawed.* (Courtesy of U.S. Army Corps of Engineers)

An overland link between Alaska and the Lower 48 had been studied, and advocated, for many years before actual construction was begun on the Alaska Highway. Two congressional commissions, one in 1933 and the other in 1940, had studied the proposed international highway. The more recent international highway commission, chaired by Washington State's Congressman Warren G. Magnuson, had enthusiastically endorsed construction of a highway to Alaska. In the June 20, 1941, *Alaska Weekly,* Magnuson was quoted as saying, "We've got to stop considering Alaska as merely an outpost and consider it an integral part of the United States. More than that, we've got to recognize it as a key to continental defense." In an earlier letter to Secretary of State Cordell Hull dated May 8, 1941, Magnuson — as chairman of the Alaskan International Highway Commission — submitted a proposed western route for the Alaska Highway and detailed arguments in favor of building the highway: Alaska's isolation; the vulnerability of Alaska's sea lanes (then the only available means of transport) to enemy attack; and the "present unpredictable, catastrophic world conditions" brought on by totalitarian force which the commission felt "we must be prepared to meet . . . ." Pointing out the proximity of Alaska to Asia, and the threat of invasion from either Russia or Japan, Magnuson noted not only the military benefit of constructing the highway, but also its value and benefits over many years, "peace or war."

The argument for defense tipped the

Left — *Whitehorse was one of the major construction camps on the Alaska Highway in 1942. The influx of thousands of men to the North had an effect on the few existing towns: a Whitehorse postal worker recalled that one day he was handling mail for 350 people, the next day for 10,000.* (Courtesy of Mrs. Earl G. Paules, reprinted from *ALASKA SPORTSMAN*®)

Above — *Tent camps provided shelter for the soldiers and civilians working on the Alaska Highway. Crews also constructed mess halls, barracks, warehouses for equipment, power, sewer, and water connections. After the war, lodges for tourists were built on some old construction camp sites.* (Courtesy of U.S. Army, reprinted from *ALASKA*® magazine)

scales in favor of building the Alaska Highway. On February 2, 1942, two months after Pearl Harbor, a special committee of the Cabinet (consisting of the Secretary of War, Secretary of the Navy, and Secretary of the Interior), along with representatives of the War Department General Staff, agreed that a highway connecting the United States and Alaska "was advisable." Approval by the Chief of Staff, U.S. Army, was given on February 6; on February 11, 1942, President Roosevelt authorized construction of the pioneer road.

Public interest in the highway, and conjecture on its route, preceded the actual authorization of the road. In July 1940, the national secretary of the Four States Highway Association wrote Alaska Governor Gruening suggesting the commission

Canada's Ian MacKenzie and Alaska's E.L. Bartlett cut the ribbon at Soldier's Summit on a blizzardy November 20, 1942, signifying completion of the Alaska Highway. Crews had raced to finish the road before the onset of winter, but much work remained on the truck trail. (Courtesy of Mrs. Earl G. Paules, reprinted from *ALASKA SPORTSMAN*®)

Above — *The first truck convoy rolled north up the Alaska Highway to Fairbanks on November 20, 1942. Steep grades, narrow widths, sharp curves, temporary bridges, unstable surfacing, and severe weather made travel hazardous and at times impossible.* (Courtesy of Mrs. Earl G. Paules, reprinted from *ALASKA SPORTSMAN®*)

Above right — *U.S. Army truck control point on the Alaska Highway in 1943. The highway opened to civilian traffic after the war and Canada's section of the road reverted to Canadian control.* (U.S. Army)

seriously consider connecting the Alaska Highway with U.S. Highway 93, "the shortest, straightest, and fastest route connecting Canada with Mexico." In an article in the November 1941 edition of *The Rotarian* entitled "That Highway to Alaska," the proposed route of the highway was shown as going west from Prince George then north up what is today the Cassiar Highway.

But the general route of the highway decided upon by the War Department in 1942, based partly on surveys made by the International Highway Commission and engineers, was along a line of existing airfields from Edmonton, Alberta, to Fairbanks, Alaska. Rights-of-way through Canada were secured by formal agreement between the two countries in March of 1942.

The massive mobilization of men and equipment necessary to construct more than a thousand miles of highway across a remote wilderness of mountains, lakes, rivers, forests, and swamps, began immediately

Some problems with the Alaska Highway, such as swampy sections turned to quicksand by rain, persisted for several years after the highway was completed. Paving and regravelling has done away with sections such as this one. (Courtesy of the U.S. Army, reprinted from *ALASKA®* magazine)

Left — *Upgrading of the Alaska Highway under way between Dawson Creek and Watson Lake. The Alaska portion of the highway is paved; the Canadian portion of the highway has some paved sections, the remainder is gravel.* (Winston Fraser)

Below — *Close-up look at the current surface of the Alaska Highway near Milepost 1304.* (David Skidmore)

after agreement was reached between Canada and the United States. Public Roads Administration offices throughout the United States tackled the task of organizing and transporting troops and civilian forces, trucks, road-building equipment, office furniture, food, tents, and other supplies north.

Colonel William Morris Hoge was assigned as commanding officer of the pioneer road project, with special responsibility for the northern section of the highway, while Colonel James A. O'Connor had command of the southern sector. Regiments of the Army Corps of Engineers, PRA engineers, and civilian contractors worked on several sections of road at the same time, trying to complete the highway before winter set in. By October, it was possible for vehicles to travel the entire length of the highway. On November 20, 1942, the Alaska-Canada Military Highway was formally dedicated at Soldier's Summit in the Yukon Territory.

But the Alaska Highway was far from complete. Work continued on the road throughout the winter of 1942-1943, in temperatures of -50°F that caused steel to break. During the summer of 1943, sections of road were resurfaced and graveled, permanent bridges installed, steep grades and sharp curves improved, and culverts and guardrails added.

The agreement between the United States and Canada on the Alaska Highway allowed that the United States would maintain the highway for the duration of the war; at the end of the war, the Canadian part of the Alaska Highway reverted to Canadian control.

As more and more civilian traffic moved up the highway after the war, lodges and other tourist facilities were built. Upgrading of the road has been an ongoing project since the highway opened, with more miles paved every year. The Alaska Highway today still has its challenges but it is a far cry from the long stretch of holes and mud travelers found in the early days.

The Story Behind the Alcan's Meandering

By Jerome F. Sheldon
Reprinted from the Fairbanks Daily News-Miner

> The
> Alaska Highway
> winding in and
> winding out
> fills my mind
> with serious doubt
> as to whether
> "the lout"
> who planned
> this route
> was going to h—!
> or coming out!
> —Anonymous

Part of the well-developed lore of the Alaska Highway, where it winds through the wilderness of the Yukon Territory, holds that its military designers deliberately planned its curves as a defense against possible Japanese strafing.

The pioneer road in 1942 was being pushed through the spruce, pine and birch forests of northwestern Canada by soldiers of the U.S. Army Corps of Engineers organized into seven different regiments. The United States and Canada had decided in February of that year to build the highway.

I was serving then as a draftee in the 18th Engineer Regiment (Combat), a force of about 1,400 men, including the band and medical detachment, that was stationed at Vancouver [Washington] Barracks, the historic Army post on the Columbia River opposite Portland. In March we knew we were to go "overseas," and rumors were rife as to our destination.

My company sailed from Seattle on Easter Sunday, April 5, 1942, aboard the gray-painted *Princess Louise*, a veteran Canadian Pacific ship of the British Columbia and Alaska service. The ship retained her C.P.R. crew, and for the next three days we enjoyed a pleasure cruise to Skagway.

There we spent five days, camped in such old buildings as the Pack Train Inn, before taking the varnished parlor cars of the White Pass & Yukon Route, the narrow-gauge railway over the mountains to Whitehorse. The regimental base camp, a huge tent city, had been established on a plateau above the town, near the airport.

"Alcan" was the Army acronym for the highway to be built, and the 18th Engineers was to work on the pioneer road heading toward the Alaskan border, more than 300 miles away.

Hardly had the snows melted in late April than the regiment's six line companies started their work. Some squads cut brush along the route, bulldozer operators "walked down" with their blades the shallow-rooted trees, and other men felled pine or spruce for rough-hewn culverts and bridges.

Various platoons and companies often worked in leap-frog fashion. They were assigned sections of a few miles each for clearing, grading and building culverts, then moved on to the head of the column.

Aerial photographs helped in choosing a route but officers relied also on "sight" engineering: someone climbing on a bulldozer with a compass and pointing in the direction the road was to take. Thus came about some of the meandering that exists in the highway today.

More than 20 years later, from a sightseeing bus driver traveling between Beaver Creek and Lake Kluane, I heard a different story. The driver said the Army had deliberately planned the curves so truck convoys wouldn't present a straight-line target for Japanese fighter planes. The driver's remarks, honed by repetition, were delivered with an air of authority. Not from me did he hear a contradiction.

The construction forces 40 years ago felt remote from the fighting fronts.

In our camps we lived in 16-foot-square tents, which we struck and re-erected with each move. We heated them with tub-like, wood-burning stoves, substituting the larger, 55-gallon fuel drums converted into wood burners during winter.

Our meals were cooked over portable gasoline ranges, and often we ate at stand-up tables made from trees cut nearby.

In the summer we wore broad-brimmed hats from which to drape mosquito netting. We were issued fur hats and parkas for winter.

As winter came on, we were still living in tents. Ice would form above our cots despite the maintenance of all-night fires. We slept in

One soldier described the wilderness the Alaska Highway crossed as "miles and miles of nothing but miles and miles." Engineers often relied on sight to route the highway, one reason for the road's meandering. (Courtesy U.S. Army, reprinted from *ALASKA®* magazine)

duck-down, double-layer sleeping bags. My regiment moved on to the Aleutian chain in January of 1943.

By official declaration, the highway was completed in October of 1943, its graveled width generally 26 feet from ditch to ditch. By then, the focus of the war against Japan had shifted from the North Pacific. The military necessity for the highway no longer existed. Most of its curves remained — to be commemorated today by a bit of postcard verse sold in gift shops along the route.

The Birth of The MILEPOST ®

By William A. "Bill" Wallace
Reprinted from ALASKA® magazine

Editor's note: *It was wartime and in a spirit of cooperation the United States and Canada joined forces to build an overland life line to link Alaska and northwestern Canada to the Lower 48. Only eight and a half months after construction began, the Alaska-Canadian (Alcan) Highway was opened on November 20, 1942. It was a primitive road, with services and accommodations hundreds of miles apart: a true challenge to the adventurous. Recognizing the need for a guide to this pioneer tote road, Bill Wallace conceived and created* The MILEPOST®. *In this article Bill Wallace tells how and why* The MILEPOST® *came into being. We offer his story and those following as a small tribute to the Alaska Highway — its builders, maintainers and travelers.*

Bill Wallace visited the Indian village of Champagne, Yukon Territory, in the early 1950s. (William Wallace)

It was on April 2, 1943, a bitterly cold night, that I had my first glimpse of the Alaska (then called the Alcan) Highway. In the next few years, I wore out several Jeeps, trucks and sedans as I drove the highway developing information and advertising and distributing my guidebook — *The MILEPOST®* — which I named after the mileage location posts that filled such a vital need along the wilderness road. But all that came later.

Dancing across the midnight sky, pale gold, violet and blue-green streamers of the northern lights intermittently silhouetted the gaunt hangars of the new army airfield at Tanacross, on the banks of Alaska's mighty Tanana River. Our small convoy of two pickup trucks, loaded with four adults, three children, food and equipment, had left Anchorage early that morning and we were dead tired, cold and hungry as we crossed the unfinished Alcan Highway and drove to the officers' quarters. There we roused a sleepy and grumpy young army captain and persuaded him to assign us a vacant KD hut until we could set up our tent, find the prerented cabin and establish our new station.

To backtrack in time: My boyhood had been spent in the small frontier seaport of Prince Rupert, not far from the Alaska border. Living in this primitive environment, I developed a love for the wilderness that time has not obliterated. I grew up and entered the newspaper and advertising profession on the West Coast, and finally wound up in New York.

To escape the martini-sodden lunches and the hectic Madison Avenue regime, my wife Helen and I decided to return to the North Country. We spent a delightful year in Homer, at the tip of the Kenai Peninsula, fishing, hunting and exploring magnificent Kachemak Bay in our 19-foot dory, powered by an ancient 9-hp outboard. It was while we were in Homer that we met Noel Routson, Homer's ranger for the Alaskan Fire Control Service (a small division of the Interior Department's General Land Office and phased out after statehood), and were it not for Noel, *The MILEPOST®* might never have been born.

Noel Routson, an experienced forester from Idaho, knew of my burning desire to travel and study the Alcan. As AFCS district supervisor at Tanacross, he wrote me regarding an opening. This was the chance I had been waiting for. After training all winter at the Anchorage headquarters, learning surveying, fire fighting and use of equipment, our two families set out for Tanacross.

Tanacross, shortened from Tanana Crossing, marked the intersection of the raw, new Alaska Highway with the historic Eagle Trail of the gold rush days. The Alaska Highway had been punched through the subarctic wilderness by the U.S. Army Corps of Engineers in less than 9 months. And now, this epic and military road was being converted to a permanent graveled highway, and our reason for being there was to prevent this wild, heavily forested region from being destroyed by fire, and to assist the lone game warden.

We were to set up an AFCS point in this once remote Indian village, and were empowered to hire Indians and, if necessary, call on the army for help in the control and fighting of fires.

Helen and I set up a wall tent with a wooden floor near the rented log cabin occupied by the Routsons. Across the still-frozen river were a few sod-roofed log cabins occupied by a tribe of Athabascan Indians, a small general store, a log church and a dispensary, operated by the Indian Bureau.

Using bluelines of the entire Alcan Highway borrowed from a highway engineer (who had partaken of some of Helen's pie and felt obligated to return the favor) and an old folder of tours offered by the Copper River &

Northwestern Railway, I made my first map, on a piece of wrapping paper, and tacked it to a wall in the Routsons' cabin. Helen and I began gathering reams of information and many North Country legends from the friendly Alaskan roadhouse owners and the hardy Canadians who were transforming construction camps into lodges along the 1,200 miles of the Alcan. All of this gave *The MILEPOST®* its local flavor.

Finally in the summer of 1948, the first edition was ready and I arranged with B.R. "Red" Kennedy, owner of Coal River Lodge at Milepost 533 to handle the ads for the Canadian section. A former Alcan construction foreman, Red knew the highway and did a wonderful job. With invaluable assistance from Bob Atwood, publisher of the *Anchorage Times,* who published the first edition in March 1949, we were on our way.

Of necessity, I was the editor, advertising man and distributor, and Helen handled the mail orders. Gradually, aided by recognition from travel editors and agencies, various offices of the AAA, as well as mentions in army publications, the demand for *The MILEPOST®* grew, and soon we were mailing copies to every corner of the globe. Color printing was unavailable in Alaska, so we went to Southern California, where former newspaper friends helped me produce a more sophisticated and handsomer guidebook.

The years passed and finally at age 61, I realized I was neglecting my lifelong avocation of oil painting, and so *The MILEPOST®* passed into the capable hands of Bob Henning, editor and publisher of *ALASKA®* magazine and owner of Alaska Northwest Publishing Company.

The MILEPOST® has flourished and grown and has become part of the unfolding destiny of the vast northwest American and Canadian wilderness.

The Alaska Highway Today

The pioneer road has changed considerably since it was built in 1942. The Alaska Highway is no longer a wilderness road. It is a highway through the wilderness. From Dawson Creek to Fairbanks, the highway stretches approximately 1,520 miles. Its length is approximate, because each summer road construction crews straighten and realign one of the pioneer road's winding sections, shaving off a mile here and a mile there. Much of the road has been paved, although there are still several hundred miles of gravel road to travel.

Communities have grown up along the highway, ranging from villages of less than a 100 people to major cities. Services for travelers are spaced about 25 to 100 miles apart along the highway. Many of these highway businesses are northern-style general stores, offering everything from propane, gas, and fishing licenses, to food, ice, a motel next door and a campground in back.

The topography of the wilderness crossed by the Alaska Highway helped determine the route of the pioneer road and is one of the

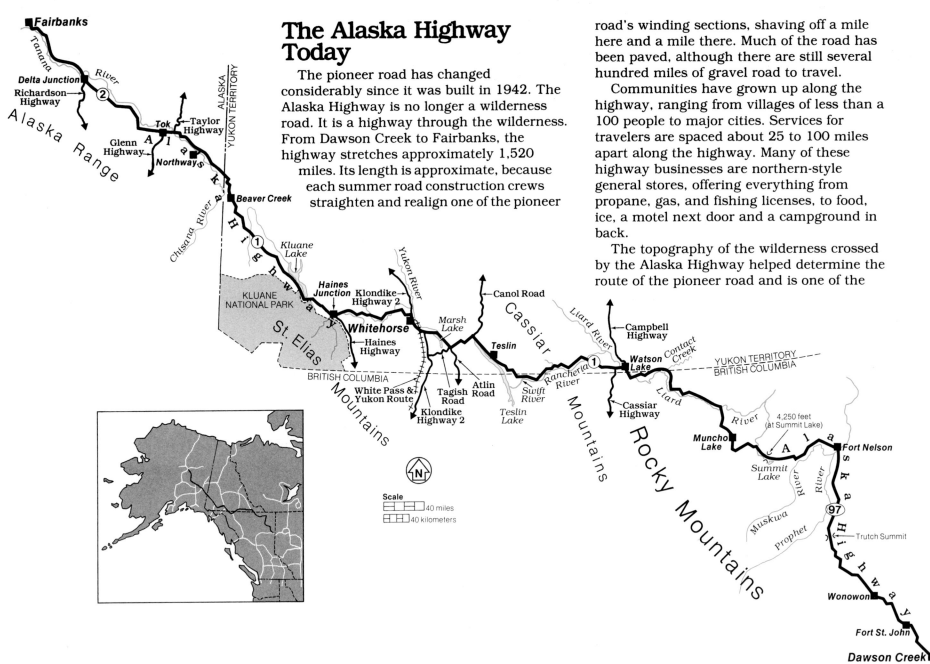

Above — *Surveyor George Mercer Dawson's report on the agricultural potential of this area led to the settlement of Dawson Creek. Construction of the Alaska Highway and oil and gas discoveries in this region have further spurred growth of the city.*
(Patrick Hawkes, staff)

Right — *The Alaska Highway curves through the rocky gorge of MacDonald Creek some 395 miles northwest of Dawson Creek. The Rocky Mountains are still covered with snow in early May.*
(Pete Martin)

Mile 0 marker for the Alaska Highway in downtown Dawson Creek. (Staff)

Deep green and blue waters of Muncho Lake, at Milepost 456, are attributed to copper oxide leaching into the lake. (Karen Donelson)

There are frequent sightings of both Stone and Dall sheep along the Alaska Highway. Stone sheep, pictured here, are darker than the white Dall sheep. (Larry Donelson)

highway's great attractions. From Dawson Creek, the Alaska Highway winds north to Fort Nelson and the foothills of the Rocky Mountains. From Fort Nelson, the highway crosses the Rocky Mountains from east to west, following canyons and crossing two divides of this great range. The highest summit on the Alaska Highway (elevation 4,250 feet) is along this section. West of the Rockies, the highway follows the Liard River into Yukon Territory and to the first stop in the Yukon for northbound travelers — Watson Lake. At Watson Lake, the Campbell Highway branches off the Alaska Highway, the first of several Yukon roads with which the Alaska Highway will connect.

The Alaska Highway continues due west from Watson Lake, following the Swift and Rancheria rivers and the shoreline of Teslin and Marsh lakes to Whitehorse, one of the biggest cities on the highway and capital of Yukon Territory. Continuing in a northwesterly direction from Whitehorse, the Alaska Highway winds up along the shore of Kluane Lake and around the back of the Saint Elias Mountains, before turning north to follow the Chisana and Tanana rivers to Fairbanks.

The images on the following pages give a glimpse of what today's Alaska Highway has to offer. The highway remains one of the truly great pioneer roads of our times.

Right — *Longest bridge on the Alaska Highway is across Nisutlin Bay, an arm of huge Teslin Lake. Sternwheel steamboats transported troops across Teslin Lake during construction of the Alaska Highway.* (Jim Whyard, reprinted from *The MILEPOST®*)

Below — *First glimpse of the mighty Liard River is at Milepost 490 on the Alaska Highway. The river heads in southcentral Yukon Territory and flows southeast into British Columbia.* (Kenneth Naversen)

Travelers add a sign at the Watson Lake sign forest, as thousands have done before them. The sign forest was started by a homesick American serviceman working on the Alaska Highway in 1942. (Sharon Paul, staff)

Liard Hot Springs at Milepost 496.5 has been a favorite spot to stop and soak since the Alaska Highway opened. (Kenneth Naversen)

55

Right — *Miles Canyon and the Robert Lowe suspension bridge south of Whitehorse can be viewed from a side road off the Alaska Highway or from a riverboat that tours the canyon in summer.* (Staff)

Above — *Old sternwheeler S.S. Klondike once plied the Yukon River. It is now permanently moored at Whitehorse.*
(Sharon Paul, staff)

Right — *View of Whitehorse, capital of Yukon Territory, from the east side of the Yukon River. The modern building at center is the Yukon Government Building.*
(Sharon Paul, staff)

Ruins of Silver City, once a trading post, roadhouse, and Royal North-West Mounted Police barracks, are at Milepost 1052. The Alaska Highway roughly parallels an old wagon road between Whitehorse and Silver City. A Public Roads Administration officer noted that the Alaska Highway often followed old trails used by Indian trappers and prospectors during its contruction in 1942. (Glen Forster)

Horses grazing in a field at the south end of Kluane Lake belong to local residents. There are few fences in this country and it is not unusual to see livestock wandering alongside — and sometimes across — the Alaska Highway. (Kenneth Naversen)

Jarvis Creek, just north of Haines Junction, is a favorite picnic and fishing spot for Alaska Highway travelers. (Sharon Paul, staff)

Sheep Mountain at Milepost 1061 was named for the Dall Sheep that reside on its rocky slopes. The Alaska Highway marks the eastern boundary of Kluane National Park between Haines Junction and Sheep Mountain.
(Karen Donelson)

Left — *Ice breaks up on Kluane Lake the last week in May or by the middle of June. This is the longest and highest lake in Yukon Territory, with an area of 154 square miles.*
(Kenneth Naversen)

Right — *The old Canadian customs station at Beaver Creek (Milepost 1202), long a source of irritation to local residents who have been plagued by flashing lights and screaming sirens whenever a tourist forgets to stop, is to be relocated.* (Sharon Paul, staff)

Fall colors on the Alaska Highway near Northway. All of the Alaska portion of the highway is paved, though severe winters, heavy traffic, and permafrost cause the pavement to buckle and heave in spots. (Pete Martin)

59

Above — *View of the scattered willows, alders, and birch, low growing spruce forests, and treeless bogs of Interior Alaska from near Milepost 1273.* (Sharon Paul, staff)

Below — *Moose rack display catches travelers' eyes at the Fortymile Roadhouse at Tetlin Junction. The Taylor Highway leads north from here to Eagle.* (Sharon Paul, staff)

Left — *Tanana River bridge at Milepost 1303.3 and a view of the Alaska Range in the distance. Alaska Highway engineers followed the course of the Tanana River north to Fairbanks.* (David Skidmore)

Above — *Tok (pronounced to rhyme with poke) was an Alaska Highway construction camp in 1942 and is now a service center for Alaska Highway travelers. The Glenn Highway to Anchorage turns off the Alaska Highway here.* (Sharon Paul, staff)

Right — *The view south along the Alaska Highway across the Johnson River bridge at Milepost 1380.5. This bridge cost approximately $650,000 to build.* (Kris Valencia, staff)

Right — *Experimental field of barley is part of a state agricultural project at Delta Junction. This view of Delta farmland and the Alaska Range is from Remington Road, a side road just off the Alaska Highway.*
(Sharon Paul, staff)

Below — *Delta barley is a key element of Alaska's agricultural development. An excellent feed for beef cattle, barley is also one of Alaska's top crops in value in sales.*
(Sharon Paul, staff)

Right — *On a clear day, the magnificent Alaska Range is visible from the Alaska Highway between Fairbanks and Delta Junction. This view is from Delta Junction, across the channeled sandy bottom of the Delta River.*
(Sharon Paul, staff)

Far right — *A monument in front of the visitor center at Delta Junction marks the official end of the Alaska Highway as it merges with the Richardson Highway to Fairbanks.* (Sharon Paul, staff)

Above — Delta Junction may be the official end of the Alaska Highway, but for many travelers Fairbanks marks the end of the long journey north from Dawson Creek. (Sharon Paul, staff)

Upper right — Fairbanks lies on the flat valley floor of the winding Tanana River. The city is bounded to the north, east, and west, by low rolling hills of birch and spruce. (Dianne Hofbeck, staff)

One of Alaska's largest sod-roofed log buildings houses North Pole's radio station KJNP. The station's two towers beam a variety of programming throughout the state and as far away as Finland. (Sharon Paul, staff)

The Chena River winds through downtown Fairbanks. This is Alaska's second largest city and unofficial capital of the Interior. (Dianne Hofbeck, staff)

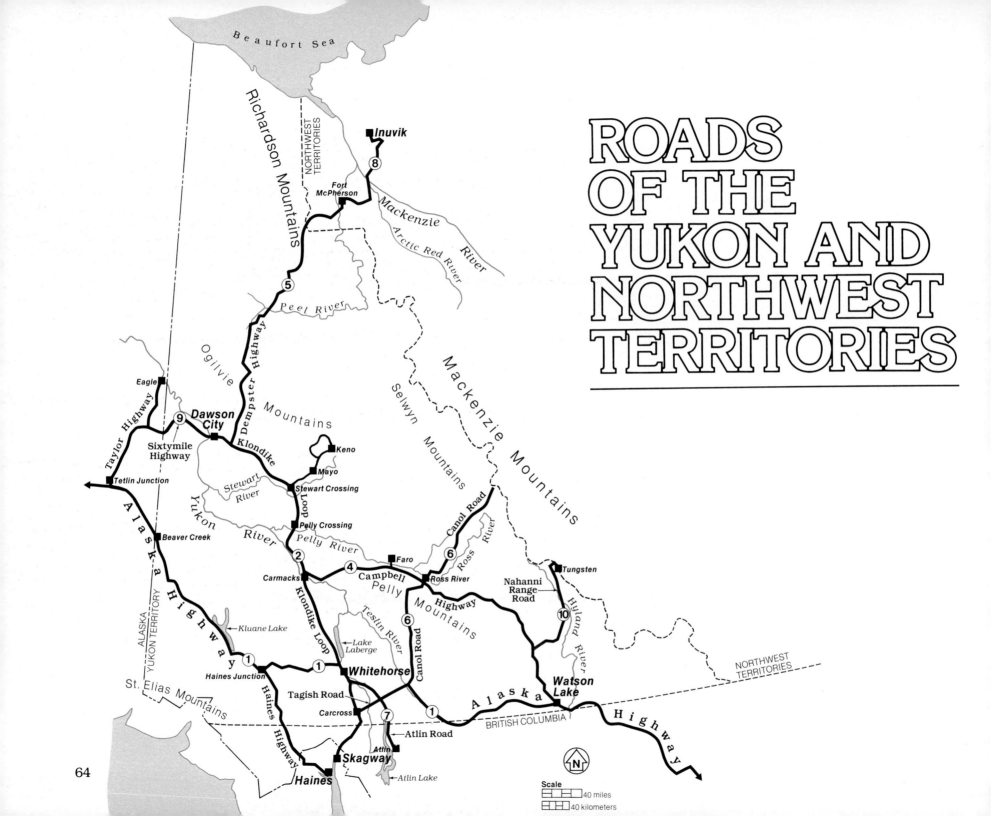

ROADS OF THE YUKON AND NORTHWEST TERRITORIES

Beaufort Sea

Inuvik

⑧

Fort McPherson

NORTHWEST TERRITORIES

Richardson Mountains

Mackenzie River

Arctic Red River

⑤

Peel River

Ogilvie Mountains

Mackenzie Mountains

Dempster Highway

Selwyn Mountains

Eagle

Taylor Highway

⑨ Dawson City

Sixtymile Highway

Klondike

Keno

Mayo

Stewart Crossing

Loop

Tetlin Junction

Stewart River

Yukon River

Pelly Crossing

Canol Road

Ross River

Tungsten

Beaver Creek

② Pelly River

Faro

④ Campbell

⑥

Ross River

Nahanni Range Road

Carmacks

Pelly

⑩

ALASKA YUKON TERRITORY

Alaska Highway

Kluane Lake

Klondike Loop

Mountains

Highway

Canol Road

Hyland River

Teslin River

⑥

NORTHWEST TERRITORIES

Lake Laberge

St. Elias Mountains

① Haines Junction

① Whitehorse

Canol Road

Watson Lake

Haines Highway

Tagish Road

Carcross

① Alaska Highway

⑦

BRITISH COLUMBIA

Atlin Road

Skagway

Atlin

Haines

Atlin Lake

Scale

40 miles
40 kilometers

64

Of the Alaska Highway's 1,520 miles, some 600 miles lie within Yukon Territory. The Alaska Highway was the first overland route to the Yukon and it remains the gateway to this immense wilderness.

Before the Alaska Highway was built, Yukon Territory's road system consisted of a few miles of old wagon roads and mining roads. The White Pass & Yukon Route railroad provided transportation from Skagway to Whitehorse, and steamships carried passengers from Whitehorse down the Yukon River to Dawson City.

Today, a half-dozen Yukon roads branch north and south from the Alaska Highway, part of a network of all-weather gravel roads leading to the far corners of Yukon Territory and up into Northwest Territories. In all, there are some 2,000 miles of road to explore: the Canol, Dempster, and Nahanni Range roads, all of which cross into Northwest Territories; the Campbell Highway; Tagish Road and Atlin Road (which leads into British Columbia); and the Klondike Highway, a loop trip from Whitehorse north to historic Dawson City and over to Alaska's Fortymile country. (Two Yukon roads, the Haines Highway and Klondike Highway 2 — both of which cross into British Columbia and Alaska — are covered in the chapter, "Sea and Land Routes to the Alaska Highway," on page 28.)

Carmacks on the Yukon River, a former riverboat stop, is 225 miles south of Dawson City on the Klondike Highway. In the 1950s, motorists crossed the Yukon by ferry here; bridges have also replaced the ferries at Pelly Crossing and Stewart Crossing. (Patrick Hawkes, staff)

Barren Ground grizzly ranges in the remote country near the end of the Canol Road. (Erwin & Peggy Bauer)

The pastime at Oldsquaw Lodge on the Canol Road in Northwest Territories is bird spotting. The lodge is situated on a tundra plain known as the Barrens, summer home to birds and caribou.
(Erwin & Peggy Bauer)

Canol Road

The bumpy, narrow Canol Road was part of the $134 million Canol Project built between 1942 and 1944, a wartime project that included an oil pipeline, refinery, airfields, pump stations, and tank farms; all part of a U.S. War Department plan to help fuel Alaska and protect it from a Japanese invasion. The more than 500 miles of gravel road, dubbed the Canadian Oil Road then shortened to Canol Road, were constructed along a pipeline to the oil fields at Norman Wells, Northwest Territories.

The Canol Project was abandoned before the end of World War II. The old Canol Road was used as a trail by hunting parties until the late 1950s, when part of the road was rebuilt and opened to summer automobile traffic. Today, the 139-mile south Canol Road between Johnson's Crossing and Ross River links the Alaska and Campbell highways. The 158 miles of the north Canol Road lead northeast from Ross River and deadend near the Tsichu River in Northwest Territories.

Right — *Rusting debris from the 1940s Canol Project — oil drums, trucks, pump stations and pipe — still litters the landscape on parts of the Canol Road.*
(Erwin & Peggy Bauer)

Below — *Sometimes called "nomads of the North," caribou roam incessantly and cover great distances. Antlers of mature bulls may reach 4 feet from base to tip.*
(Erwin & Peggy Bauer)

Above — *Lake trout are plentiful in Northwest Territories waters. Lakes and streams along the Canol also support grayling and northern pike.* (Erwin & Peggy Bauer)

67

First view of Yukon River for Campbell Highway travelers is about 16 miles from the road's junction with the Klondike Highway. (Patrick Hawkes, staff)

Campbell Highway

Yukon Highway 4 was named for Robert Campbell of the Hudson's Bay Company, the first white man to penetrate the central Yukon, and the man who discovered and named the Pelly River (for Hudson's Bay Company governor Sir John Henry Pelly). A major tributary of the Yukon River, the Pelly flows beside the highway for almost 100 miles. The highway, 365 miles of gravel road, crosses and follows dozens of rivers and streams as it winds north from Watson Lake through the central Yukon, connecting the Alaska Highway with the Klondike Highway. Completed in the late 1960s, the Campbell Highway linked Watson Lake with the old settlement of Ross River and the newer mining town of Faro.

Nahanni Range Road

The Nahanni Range Road branches off the Campbell Highway some 66 miles north of Watson Lake. Designated Yukon Highway 10, this 125-mile gravel road to the tungsten mine in Northwest Territories is used primarily by mining trucks. The road ends at the community of Tungsten in Northwest Territories, the company town for Canada Tungsten Mining Corporation Limited.

Nahanni Range Road, also called Tungsten Road, crosses Yukon border into Northwest Territories to the mining town of Tungsten. The rough gravel road branches off the Campbell Highway 66 miles north of Watson Lake. (Richard Harrington, reprinted from ALASKA GEOGRAPHIC®)

Tagish Road

Yukon Highway 8, the Tagish Road, leads south from the Alaska Highway to the small community of Tagish on the Tagish (also called Six Mile) River, between Marsh and Tagish lakes. This 33-mile road joins with Klondike Highway 2 at Carcross.

Tagish Lake, a huge body of water straddling the Yukon-British Columbia border near the small community of Tagish, was an important water route for early gold seekers. (Richard Harrington, reprinted from *ALASKA GEOGRAPHIC®*)

Atlin Road

Designated Yukon Highway 7, the road to Atlin was under construction when the first edition of *The MILEPOST®* was published in 1949, and completed the following year. Today, the 61-mile gravel road to the once-isolated pioneer gold mining town of Atlin is a popular hour-and-a-half side trip from the Alaska Highway. About midway on the drive the road passes the north shore of 90-mile-long Atlin Lake and crosses into British Columbia. The village of Atlin, at the end of Atlin Road, overlooks the clear water of huge Atlin Lake and the spectacular mountains of this far corner of British Columbia.

Above — *View of the village of Atlin on Atlin Lake from the town's mineral springs gazebo.* (Robert D. Hahn, reprinted from *The MILEPOST®*)

Below — *S.S. Tarahne on the beach at Atlin carried passengers and freight between Atlin and Scotia Bay until 1936.* (Steve Owlett)

Dempster Highway

In an isolated corner of the Yukon, a rough gravel road cuts a lonely path north across the Ogilvie and Richardson mountains to the Mackenzie River delta of Northwest Territories. This is the Dempster Highway, a 451-mile stretch of road completed in 1978 and designated Yukon Highway 5 for its first 285 miles, and Northwest Territories Highway 8 for the last 166 miles.

Left — *Bone-jarring Dempster Highway snakes across the lonely wilderness between Dawson City, Yukon Territory, and Inuvik, Northwest Territories.* (Robert D. Jones)

Above — *Old grave site along the Dempster Highway in the Ogilvie Mountains north of Dawson City. The mountain range was named for William Ogilvie, a Klondike surveyor noted for his honest and impartial decisions.* (Larry Donelson, reprinted from The MILEPOST®)

Left — *Igloo Church in Inuvik is painted to simulate snow blocks.* (Glen Forster)

Above — *Pastel-colored houses have earned Inuvik the nickname "Easter Egg Town."* (Glen Forster)

Right — *View of the Tombstone Range and the valley of the North Fork Klondike River about 42 miles up the Dempster Highway.* (Larry Donelson)

The Dempster begins at the Klondike Highway, a few miles south of Dawson City, and ends at Inuvik, Northwest Territories, the largest Canadian community north of the Arctic Circle. There is little of civilization along this road; mostly there is wildlife, clear streams and rivers, rolling hills, high mountains, and arctic tundra meadow.

Fort McPherson is the second largest settlement along the highway (population about 820). Buried in the cemetery outside the Anglican church here are Inspector Fitzgerald and three other men of the Royal North-West Mounted Police. These four were lost on a patrol to Dawson City in the winter of 1910-1911. Their bodies were recovered by Corporal W.J.D. Dempster of the Mounties on March 22, 1911.

Arctic Red River ferry crossing on the Dempster is one of two such crossings on the highway.
(Larry Donelson, reprinted from *The MILEPOST®*)

71

Klondike Loop

In 1950, a 245-mile road was built connecting the United Keno Hill Mining Company at Mayo with the Alaska Highway. By 1955, the Mayo Road had been upgraded for automobile traffic, and another 123 miles of road from Stewart Crossing to Dawson City completed. The 1956 edition of *The MILEPOST*® logged the Dawson-Mayo Road as an alternate loop trip to Alaska via Dawson City. Today, this route is referred to in *The MILEPOST*® as the Klondike Loop, a 500-mile drive from the Alaska Highway

Dawson City, capital of Yukon Territory until 1953, is located at the confluence of the Yukon and Klondike rivers. A free car ferry crosses the Yukon here for Alaska-bound travelers. (John Johnson)

north to Dawson City, then west into Alaska and back to the Alaska Highway.

The loop drive begins on the Klondike Highway (Yukon Highway 2) at its turnoff on the Alaska Highway just north of Whitehorse. The first 213 miles of the Klondike Highway, part of the old Mayo Road, pass Lake Laberge, Carmacks, and Pelly Crossing to Stewart Crossing. Here, the Mayo Road (now Yukon Highway 11) cuts off northeast to Mayo, Elsa, and Keno, while the Klondike Highway continues 114 miles northwest to Dawson City.

Dawson City's population today is about 900; in 1898, the population was an estimated 30,000. The city dates from the 1896 discovery of gold on a Klondike River tributary named Rabbit Creek (later renamed

Above left — *Parade through downtown Dawson City is part of Discovery Days celebration. This Yukon holiday commemorates the Klondike gold discovery of August 17, 1896.*
(Winston Fraser)

Above — *Dawson City turns out to celebrate Independence Day in 1900. Klondikers made up for the long cold winters by celebrating holidays, arrivals, departures, and just about anything else in summer.*
(Kinsey & Kinsey, reprinted from *Klondike Lost*)

Visitors try panning for gold at Poverty Bar Placers on Bonanza Creek Road.
(Patrick Hawkes, staff)

Right — *Sweeping the gold out of the riffles or slats of the sluice box was part of spring cleanup in the Klondike in 1903.* (Kinsey & Kinsey photo, reprinted from *Klondike Lost*)

Below — *Dredge Number 4 on Bonanza Creek Road was built by the Yukon Gold Company in 1908. These huge dredges mechanized gold mining in the Klondike, a necessary step to extract the shrinking supply of gold, but one which put crews of miners out of work.*
(Patrick Hawkes, staff)

Bonanza Creek). When news of the find leaked out to the rest of the world, the greatest gold rush in history began.

Thousands of gold seekers arrived in Dawson City, most following the Trail of '98 from Skagway over the mountains to Lakes Lindeman and Bennett, then down the Yukon River to Dawson City. (The Klondike Highway, which begins in Skagway, parallels this old gold rush route.) In 1900, Dawson City was the largest Canadian city west of Winnipeg. By 1903, the boom had ended as gold strikes in Nome and elsewhere drew away many of Dawson's citizens.

The boardwalks and gravel streets, turn-of-the-century buildings and entertainments of Dawson City draw hundreds of visitors up the Klondike Highway today. Alaska-bound travelers continue west from Dawson across the Yukon River via a government-operated ferry.

From the Yukon River crossing, the Sixtymile Highway — also called the Dawson-Boundary Road (Yukon Highway 9) — crosses into Alaska. An old mining road, this 60-mile gravel road across the mountains and valleys of the Yukon-Alaska border is often referred to as the ''Top of the World Highway.'' It ends at its junction with the Taylor Highway, which leads south to the Alaska Highway.

Left — *Boundary, Alaska, first stop across the border on the Sixtymile Highway from Dawson City.* (Sharon Paul, staff)

Below — *The sixty miles of road between Dawson City, Yukon Territory, and Boundary, Alaska, is sometimes called the "Top of the World Highway."* (Sharon Paul, staff)

ROAD BUILDING IN ALASKA

Early-Day Autos on Alaska's First Roads

By Terrence Cole

Many of the major highways in Alaska today follow the routes of gold rush trails that were blazed by prospectors, military explorers, and scientists at the turn of the century. Men on foot, or with horses, dogs, canoes, and poling boats, charted the mountain passes and river systems of the Alaskan wilderness, and identified the transportation routes that are today followed by the Richardson Highway, the Taylor Highway, and other modern roads in Alaska.

Only with the coming of the First World War did the dog and the horse begin to give

An early-day automobile road up the Nome River valley, on the Seward Peninsula. (Lomen Family Collection, University of Alaska Archives, Fairbanks)

way to the "benzine buggy." But for many years after that, Alaskan roads remained treacherous for man, beast, and machine alike, and only in the 1920s did automobiles gain widespread popularity in Alaska. Bumpy corduroy roads paved with spruce poles laid sideways across the swampy tundra often disappeared in the bog, leaving the horse-drawn wagon or Model T that attempted to drive over the trail stranded in axle-deep mud. Then, as now, one of the major problems in constructing roads in the North was building across permafrost, permanently frozen ground. It was found necessary to lay an insulating layer of brush and poles over the top of the moss, and keep adding to the road bed as it gradually sank into the slowly melting ground beneath it.

In lands farther to the south, roads could be built by simply scraping away the surface vegetation, but in the North that proved disastrous. "It has been the universal

"Alaskans and the Alaska Road Commission have long recognized the fact that the development of the Territory is related to — indeed is dependent upon — the development of adequate overland transportation facilities. The first session of the Legislature of Alaska, convened 42 years ago in 1913, memorialized the Congress of the United States to develop a highway network. The demand for roads — and even more roads — has been continuous to this day."

—from the 1955 Report of the Alaska Road Commission

Seated on the right of the Thomas Flyer, the first automobile in Nome, is General A.W. Greely, the famous arctic explorer, on his visit to Alaska in 1905. The crank of the Flyer is visible on the front of the car, tied to the shock absorber. (F.H. Nowell, courtesy of the University of Washington Historical Photograph Collection)

experience," a geologist wrote about road construction in 1905, "that wherever the moss is cut into, thawing immediately commences, and the trail which was passable becomes a filthy, slimy mass of mud, roots, and broken stone, a difficult route for men on foot, a slow and tiresome road for loaded animals, and an impassable obstacle to any sort of vehicle." Occasionally horses became so stuck in the muck that they had to be pulled out with ropes or shot.

Another hazard for early travelers were river crossings. Fording glacial streams could be a tricky affair, but every Alaskan had to master the art, since none but the largest rivers were spanned by bridges or ferries. Winter travel had its own dangers, but because the rivers and the land were frozen, overland trips were often much easier during the coldest months of the year. It was a long time, however, before automobile drivers learned how to keep a car running at 50 below in the Interior of Alaska.

With such poor roads in Alaska 70 years

When the Thomas Flyer, the American entry in the round-the-world race from New York to Paris, stopped in Valdez in April 1908, the whole town turned out to greet the car. Four well-dressed women posed in the car for the photographer. The vehicle was equipped with two 20-foot-long wooden skid planks on either side of the car, instead of fenders, as well as tanks of extra gasoline, camping equipment, spare parts, tow ropes, and survival gear. When the road through Thompson Pass proved impassable, the crew of the Flyer gave up the idea of trying to drive across Alaska from Valdez to Nome, and the route of the race was changed, with the car being shipped directly to Siberia by steamship. (Anchorage Historical and Fine Arts Museum)

The first roads in Alaska were often rough, rocky trails. This road around Cape Nome, one of the first automobile roads in Alaska, was under construction in the summer and fall of 1905. It appears that a weary traveler may have abandoned his suitcase on the side of the road.
(Carrie M. McLain Memorial Museum)

ago, the vehicles that traveled them had to be versatile. "When it rains in Alaska," a newspaper reported in 1915, "the bottom falls out of what they call roads, and the automobile becomes a submarine."

The first automobiles in Alaska arrived shortly after the gold rush. In Skagway in 1905, Bobby Sheldon made an automobile from scratch, without ever having seen a motorcar before. Using a photograph that he had seen in a popular science magazine, he built a two-passenger, box-like car with buggy wheels, a friction clutch, and a one-cylinder, two-cycle marine engine, that had a top speed of about 15 miles an hour. Though he seldom drove his homemade car at night, the car was equipped with two carbide miner's lamps for driving in the dark. Sheldon's unique car, which was once written up in Ripley's "Believe It or Not," has for many years been a featured exhibit at the University of Alaska Museum in Fairbanks.

Other mechanically minded Alaskans like

Bobby Sheldon at the stick of the handcrafted automobile that he built at Skagway in 1905. He salvaged the engine from a small motor launch that had sunk in Skagway harbor and the wheels were driven by a bicycle chain.
(Dedman photo, courtesy of R.N. De Armond)

Fort Davis, was probably the first "automobile road" in Alaska.

When the two-mile stretch was completed, the *Nome News* said it was a highway which "leaves many thoroughfares in the states way behind," and the paper announced, "one may, for the first time in Nome's history, take an afternoon's ramble on a level pathway through the tundra." But the automobile held even more promise for the future.

"Automobiles are now used in London and other cities where streets are narrow and crooked," the Nome newspaper stated, so why not in Alaska? In addition, the cars would be cheap to operate. "The cost of running one of these machines will be very much less than that of operating a small railroad," the editor noted, "only one man being required for each car and one gallon of gasoline used in every five miles."

Despite such good gas mileage, it was incredibly expensive to construct roads in Alaska, and it took many years for barely passable roads to be built in the territory, as the organizers and contestants of the 1908 New York to Paris automobile race discovered.

The New York to Paris auto race in 1908 has been called "the most thrilling event in the early history of the automobile," as six cars attempted to drive around the world. Sponsored jointly by the *New York Times* and *Le Matin* of Paris, the organizers admitted that the hardest part of the round-the-world race would probably be through Alaska, but the racers believed that

Sheldon built their own automobiles, but those who could afford them usually bought factory-built models. One of the earliest factory-made autos in Alaska was a seven-passenger Thomas Flyer that the Alaska Automobile Transportation Company shipped to Nome in 1905, the same year that Sheldon was tinkering with his invention in Skagway. The Flyer was "capable of a high rate of speed," and was to be used by the transportation company to haul passengers from Nome to Solomon. The company planned to build its own toll road between the two cities, and though it never finished the road, a portion was completed. A two-mile stretch of narrow gravel road that the company built in 1905 between Nome and

they could drive on the "frozen roads" of the North in the wintertime from Valdez to Nome, and then drive across the ice of the Bering Strait to Siberia. After driving across the country from New York to San Francisco, the automobiles would be shipped north to Valdez on a steamer where they would race some 1,000 miles through the Alaskan wilderness, in a land where there were no roads and few automobiles had ever gone before.

In those days any automobile trip was an adventure, and driving across the continent the racers battled blizzards, floods, and desert heat. On the roads between New York and Albany one of the German drivers complained, "I wish we were now in Alaska, for it will surely be easier and pleasanter going than this."

The first car to be shipped north to Valdez was the American entry, a Thomas Flyer, the same make of automobile that had been used earlier in Nome. When the Flyer arrived in Valdez the whole town turned out to greet the car, and cheered as it drove off the dock. However, there were several serious problems. The driver discovered that the "road" from Valdez to Fairbanks over which he was supposed to drive, which is today the Richardson Highway, was barely passable in 1908 for horse-drawn sleds, and in places on the trail a single horse could hardly move without falling off the side of a mountain. The driver carefully measured the trail and found that at the widest the beaten down path through the snow was only 45 inches, while the automobile had a wheelspan of 56 inches. Although the snowbanks in Valdez were still 15 feet deep, it was already April and the spring thaw had begun. One step off the trail and a man would sink in the snow up to his waist.

Right — *A long-distance trip on an Alaskan highway 70 years ago was no small undertaking. Ready for a rough ride over the Richardson Highway to Valdez, a crowd watches as the Gibson Auto stage line prepares to leave from the front of the Nordale Hotel in Fairbanks.* (Historical Photo Collection, University of Alaska Archives, Fairbanks)

Below — *An automobile was always an attraction in early-day Alaska. Here, a group of Eskimos pose behind the wheel of a four-door luxury car, probably the seven-passenger Thomas Flyer that was shipped to Nome in 1905 to be used as a limousine between Nome and Solomon.* (F.H. Nowell, courtesy of the University of Washington Historical Photograph Collection)

Deciding that it was "utterly impossible" to drive across Alaska or even get more than one mile past Valdez without being buried in a snowdrift, the route of the New York to Paris race was changed to leave out the stretch from Valdez to Nome, and the cars were taken instead by ship to Vladivostok. Though it had been delayed by stopping in Valdez, the Thomas Flyer eventually won the race from New York to Paris, reaching there in late July, and becoming at that time the most famous automobile in the world.

It is easier to drive across Alaska today than it was in 1908. Motorists who travel on modern roads in Alaska don't have to equip their cars with 20-foot-long wooden skid planks on either side of the vehicle, or install a removable top "similiar to those used on the old prairie schooners," as the drivers of the Thomas Flyer did. Thanks in part to the efforts of the Alaska Road Commission, the agency that constructed and maintained public roads, trails, and other facilities in the territory from 1905 to 1956, Alaska's primitive road system gradually expanded year by year. The Bureau of Public Roads, which some Alaskans referred to as the Bureau of Parallel Ruts, replaced the Road Commission in 1956, when federal aid to highways was extended to Alaska for the first time.

The Road Commission was under the jurisdiction of the War Department until the 1930s, and the Army carried out most of the road surveys and other explorations. In those early years they examined and surveyed almost every important transportation route in Alaska, and by 1932 had constructed about 500 miles of low-standard roads in the territory, and nearly 10,000 miles of trails and sled roads. Given the great expense in building roads in the north, and the distances to be covered, their achievement was remarkable. As one writer stated in 1913, "Laboring under the difficulties of a short season and the greater difficulty of transporting supplies, the road commission has worked wonders in a wilderness."

Alaska's chief road builder in the early part of this century was Major Wilds P. Richardson, the first head of the Alaska Road Commission, and the man for whom the Richardson Highway is named. Richardson is shown here with a group of other military officers, Road Commission officials, and dignitaries, in Valdez in 1909. Richardson is sitting on the far right in the backseat of a White Steamer, his face partly obscured by the driver's hat. Like many early American automobiles, the steering wheel of the White Steamer was on the right side of the car. (R.N. De Armond)

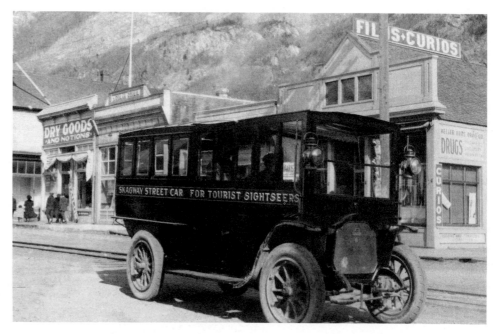

The Skagway Street Car for Tourist Sightseers cruised up and down the streets of Skagway in the mid-1920s. (Dedman photo, courtesy of R.N. De Armond)

Clockwise from above — *Old Rapids Hunting Lodge, described as the "farthest north of the old-time Richardson trail hostelries" in the 1955 edition of* The MILEPOST®, *is near Black Rapids Glacier on the Richardson Highway.* (Sharon Paul, staff)

Oldest existing roadhouse in Alaska, and still operating in the original building, is the Sourdough Roadhouse at Milepost 147.5 on the Richardson Highway. (Third Eye Photography)

Gakona Lodge on the Glenn Highway was placed on the National Register of Historic Places in 1977. The original carriage house is now a restaurant. (Pete Martin)

Paxson Lodge, at the junction of the Richardson and Denali highways, was established in 1903. (Third Eye Photography)

Old Slana Roadhouse on the Nabesna Road is now a private home. (Sharon Paul, staff)

84

ROADHOUSES

A footnote in some early editions of *The MILEPOST®* defined roadhouse:

ROADHOUSE — *In Alaska, this term derives from those early-day hostelries along the trails used by dog-team, horse-drawn sled and wagon stage. Today it means the same as lodge or hotel.*

Early roadhouses were spaced about a day's travel (by horse or dog) apart and offered travelers the basic amenities: food

and shelter. There were hundreds of these roadhouses in the early days of the territory; most have vanished, their exact locations unknown. Some were destroyed and new structures built on the old site. The famous Blix Roadhouse, destroyed in the early 1930s, has been replaced by the Copper Center Lodge. Other roadhouses have survived, with some rebuilding over the years: Gakona Roadhouse, Sourdough Lodge, Paxson Lodge, and Talkeetna Roadhouse, among others.

Roadhouses, inns, lodges, hotels and motels are scattered along Alaska's roads today, and food and shelter are no longer a day's hard journey away by horse-drawn rig or dog team. But modern motorists may share, somewhat, the same feeling of relief that early-day travelers must have felt when — tired of traveling — they saw a light in the distance that meant dinner and a bed for the night.

Left — *Talkeetna Roadhouse offers the same thing early-day roadhouses offered — food and lodging.* (Sharon Paul, staff)

Above — *Old Richardson Roadhouse has housed many different businesses over the years; it was last a bar.* (Pete Martin)

85

RICHARDSON HIGHWAY

The Richardson Highway was Alaska's first road, connecting Fairbanks in the Interior with tidewater at Valdez. It began as a trail for the gold stampeders of 1898, was later converted to a wagon road, and in 1913 was driven by an enterprising Alaskan named Bobby Sheldon in a Model T Ford. It has been open to vehicle traffic for more than 60 years.

It was the Klondike gold rush of 1897-1898 that brought men to Valdez. Of the thousands of gold seekers bound for the Klondike in '98, most came through Skagway and Dyea over the Chilkoot and White Pass trails, arduous but established routes to the Yukon gold fields. The unlucky ones came by less well-known routes, such as the Valdez trail. Advertised as the all-American route to the Klondike, the Valdez trail led from the port of Valdez up over Valdez Glacier, down the Klutina River

Worthington Glacier spills down mountainside to within a few hundred yards of the highway. This view of the glacier is from Milepost 29 on the Richardson Highway. (Sharon Paul, staff)

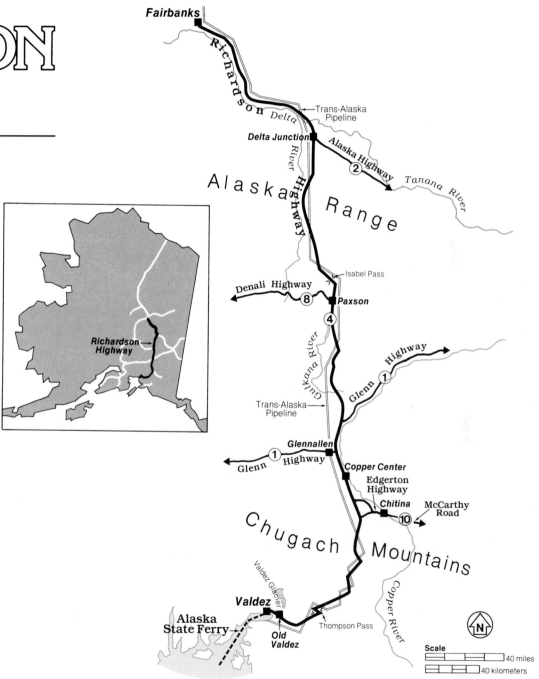

Old Valdez, at the foot of Valdez Glacier. This was the location of the townsite until the 1964 earthquake destroyed the community. (P.S. Hunt photo, reprinted from *The Copper Spike*)

to the Copper River, then northeast to Mentasta Pass, the Fortymile River, and Eagle. From the thriving gold rush town of Eagle, the route followed the Yukon River to the Klondike gold fields.

Valdez Glacier was as far as many of the gold stampeders got on the Valdez to Eagle trail. The deadly glacier took its toll as men were turned back by exhaustion, scurvy, and snow blindness. Witnessing the struggle of these early pioneers was Captain William R. Abercrombie of the 2nd U.S. Infantry, the man whose work on the trail would earn it the appellation "Abercrombie Trail."

Abercrombie, who had led the Copper River exploring expedition in 1884, arrived in Valdez in 1898 with a company of 20

men, under orders to explore the Valdez to Eagle trail. Lieutenant P.G. Lowe of his company traversed the trail as far as Mentasta Pass. A year later, Abercrombie returned with orders to construct a military road from Valdez, where Fort Liscum was to be established, to Eagle, where the U.S. Army was building Fort Egbert.

Instead of crossing Valdez Glacier, Abercrombie's route — like today's Richardson Highway — went up through Keystone Canyon and over Thompson Pass. At the fork of the Copper and Gulkana rivers (near the present-day junction with the Glenn Highway), Abercrombie's route cut northeast to Eagle, paralleling what is today the Tok Cutoff and Taylor Highway.

Present-day Valdez, located four miles west of the old townsite, is backed by the Chugach Mountains to the north. (Sharon Paul, staff)

Right — *Freight sleds at summit of Thompson Pass, circa 1910. The Alaska Road Commission recorded 3,500 persons and 2,480 tons of freight moved over the Richardson trail in 1910.* (Guy F. Cameron photo, reprinted from *The Copper Spike*)

Below — *View south in early fall from top of Thompson Pass of the Lowe River valley and surrounding Chugach Mountains.* (Sharon Paul, staff)

Left — *Copper Center on the Klutina River, originally a mining camp and Indian village, is now a trade and service center on the Richardson Highway with a population of about 150.* (Sharon Paul, staff)

Below — *Old log jail at Copper Center was still in use in 1949 when* The MILEPOST® *described it as "so clean and comfortable, and which supplies its inmates with such wholesome food," that those confined for minor offenses "seem to enjoy the change."* (Sharon Paul, staff)

Although the Klondike gold rush waned, the military kept the trail open. In 1903, the U.S. Army Signal Corps finished laying the trans-Alaska telegraph line along the route between Fort Liscum and Fort Egbert. That same year, word of the 1902 Fairbanks gold strike started another stampede up the trail, this time from Valdez to Fairbanks.

The Valdez to Fairbanks trail remained an important route to the Interior, and by 1910 the rough trail — once suitable only for packtrains in summer and dog teams in winter — had been converted to a wagon road. The work was done under the direction of General Wilds P. Richardson, first

Below — *Richardson Highway between Paxson and Delta Junction, an 80-mile stretch of road, cuts across the Alaska Range.* (Sharon Paul, staff)

Right — *Trailer camped at Summit Lake is dwarfed by Gulkana Glacier beyond. The glacier is perched on 8,000-foot Icefall Peak.*
(Betty Johannsen)

Wild flowers are abundant along the Richardson Highway in June. Frigid arnica (top photo), one of Alaska's most common low-growing arnicas, is found along gravelly roadsides. Dwarf fireweed (lower photo) is widespread throughout the state, found along rivers, on hillsides and roadsides.
(Both photos by Sharon Paul, staff)

president of the Alaska Road Commission, for whom the highway is named. The ARC updated the road to automobile standards in the 1920s and continued to improve the road with new bridges, widening and rerouting, finally hard-surfacing the highway in 1957.

Today's Richardson Highway (Alaska Route 4) is a modern, paved, two-lane highway open all year to vehicle traffic. The highway follows the routes of Abercrombie and Richardson up through Keystone Canyon, cresting the Chugach Mountains at 2,771-foot Thompson Pass. North from its junction with the Glenn Highway, the Richardson crosses the Alaska Range at 3,000-foot Isabel Pass, before descending into Delta Junction, where it joins the Alaska Highway into Fairbanks.

Traces of the past remain along the Richardson. Keystone Canyon, the Lowe River, Thompson Pass: All were named by Captain Abercrombie. Near Milepost 15 of the present highway is a hand-drilled railroad tunnel, all that remains of a proposed railroad from Valdez to the Interior that was begun, then abandoned, in 1906. Between Mileposts 13 and 16, sections of the early wagon road — a precipitous goat path along the sides of the Chugach Mountains — are still visible. But dominating the scenery along much of the Richardson Highway are not relics of the past, but the high

technology of today. The trans-Alaska oil pipeline, which stretches 800 miles from Prudhoe Bay to the marine terminal at Valdez, parallels the length of the 368-mile Richardson Highway. Visible from the road are the pipeline, pump stations, and abandoned work camps from pipeline construction days.

The Richardson Highway remains a vital link between Valdez, with its ice-free port, and Fairbanks, offering the shortest link to much of the Interior for seaborne cargo. The Richardson junctions with the Alaska Highway, Denali Highway, and Glenn Highway. From the end of the Richardson at Valdez, the state ferry system provides passenger and vehicle transport to Cordova and across Prince William Sound to the Kenai Peninsula.

Left — *Lowe River flows west through Keystone Canyon. Captain W.R. Abercrombie named both the river and canyon.* (Jon R. Nickles)

Below — *Hand-drilled tunnel near Milepost 15 was part of a 1906 effort to build a railroad through Keystone Canyon.* (Sharon Paul, staff)

Above — *Port Valdez on Prince William Sound, the most northerly ice-free port in the Western Hemisphere, is marine terminal for the trans-Alaska pipeline. First tanker load of oil from the North Slope departed Valdez in 1977.* (Sharon Paul, staff)

Right — *Alaska state ferry Bartlett departs Valdez with passengers and vehicles bound for Cordova and Whittier.* (Sharon Paul, staff)

Copper River Highway sweeps east from Cordova across the sloughs and channels of the Copper River Delta. The Copper River empties into the Gulf of Alaska.
(Sharon Paul, staff)

COPPER RIVER HIGHWAY

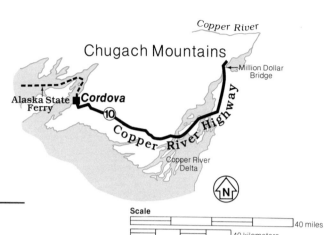

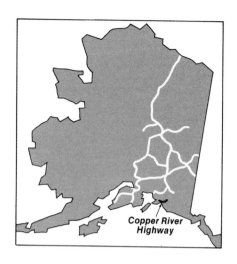

Scale

40 miles

40 kilometers

The Copper River Highway leads east from Cordova across the sloughs and channels of the Copper River Delta to the Million Dollar Bridge, some 48 miles from town, and there the highway abruptly ends. It is Alaska's great unfinished highway, since 1941 a proposed link between Cordova and Chitina.

Like the Richardson Highway, the history of the Copper River Highway began with the gold and copper discoveries in Alaska at the turn of the century. Talk of a railroad from the Gulf of Alaska to the Interior started as early as 1898, but the task was a formidable one: rugged terrain, severe winters, and the logistical problems of providing men and supplies to build a railroad seemed overwhelming. But further discoveries of copper and coal provided a profitable incentive for a railway, and survey of a possible route began in earnest.

Fierce competition followed among the port cities of Valdez, Katalla, and Eyak for the proposed railway which would link the

Building a bridge across the Copper River flats in 1908 for the Copper River & Northwestern Railway was just one of many formidable engineering tasks during construction of the railroad. (E.A. Hegg photo, Alaska Historical Library, reprinted from *The Copper Spike*)

Above — *Originally a small fishing village called Eyak, the town of Cordova developed between 1906 and 1910 with the coming of the CR&NW railway. This photo shows First Avenue under construction in 1908.* (Alaska Historical Library, reprinted from *The Copper Spike*)

Right — *Downtown Cordova today. The Prince William Sound fishery and local fish processing plants support many of the city's 2,223 residents.* (Sharon Paul, staff)

rich Kennecott copper mines with tidewater. The small cannery community of Eyak on Prince William Sound, which was to become Cordova, was finally chosen as the railhead. Construction of the Copper River & Northwestern Railway began in 1908. The CR&NW was engineered by M.J. Heney, builder of the White Pass & Yukon Route railroad, and owned and operated by the powerful Guggenheim-J.P. Morgan Alaska Syndicate.

The 194 miles of track connecting Cordova to the Kennecott Mine were completed in 1911, and the CR&NW operated until 1938, when both the mine and railway ceased operation.

In 1941, the Guggenheim-J.P. Morgan syndicate transferred the CR&NW right-of-way to the federal government (surprisingly, free of charge) with the stipulation that it be used as a public highway.

Construction of the Copper River Highway along the old CR&NW railbed began in 1945, with the U.S. Forest Service completing 13 miles of roadway. Road building continued, slowly, until 1958, when the highway reached the Million Dollar Bridge at Mile 48. Engineers found the old railroad bridge in good shape, and replaced the old decking with concrete for vehicle traffic. By 1963, 50 miles of gravel road were open to the bridge and another 9 miles past Abercrombie Rapids were under construction. A year earlier, Cordova had been linked to Valdez by auto ferry for the first time.

Million Dollar Bridge cost $1.5 million to build in 1910. The north span of the bridge collapsed during the 1964 earthquake.
(Sharon Paul, staff)

On March 27, 1964, the most destructive earthquake ever recorded in North America struck Alaska's central region. The earthquake, which registered between 8.4 and 8.6 on the Richter scale, severely damaged the roadbed of the Copper River Highway. The quake also knocked the northern truss span of the Million Dollar Bridge into the Copper River and distorted the remaining spans. Since 1964, the Copper River Highway has remained the proposed link to Chitina.

The future of the Copper River Highway is uncertain. A new steel and concrete structure could replace the Million Dollar Bridge in the near future, paving the way for completing the proposed link to the Richardson Highway. The 48 miles of existing highway have been upgraded and the 12 miles of pavement from Cordova may be extended (the remaining 36 miles are gravel).

The Copper River Highway provides access to the Copper River Delta, one of the great bird-watching areas in Alaska. The delta is an important nesting and breeding area for dusky Canada geese, trumpeter swans, and other birds. At the end of the highway is Childs Glacier, one of a half-dozen glaciers in Alaska accessible by road.

Above — *Spectacular face of Childs Glacier on west side of Copper River. The glacier was named by Captain W.R. Abercrombie during his 1884 Copper River exploration for a Philadelphia gentleman named George Childs.*
(Sharon Paul, staff)

Right — *A trumpeter swan, one of the largest of all North American waterfowl. Great numbers of these swans concentrate along the Copper River and its tributaries.*
(Tom Ulrich, reprinted from *A Guide to the Birds of Alaska*)

Far right — *Glacially silted waters of the Copper River Delta. The delta is one of the most important bird migration routes in Alaska.*
(Sharon Paul, staff)

Near Milepost 0 of the Edgerton Highway. The 33-mile-long highway leads east across the Copper River valley to Chitina. In the distance is 14,163-foot Mount Wrangell. (Sharon Paul, staff)

EDGERTON HIGHWAY
and the
McCarthy Road

The 33-mile Edgerton Highway — known locally as the Edgerton Cutoff — roughly parallels an old pack trail that connected the Valdez to Fairbanks trail (now the Richardson Highway) with Chitina, once an important rail stop on the Copper River & Northwestern Railway. Beyond Chitina, the rugged McCarthy Road, a 63-mile extension of the Edgerton, follows the abandoned railroad bed of the CR&NW to McCarthy and the Kennecott copper mines.

Construction of the Copper River & Northwestern Railway, linking Cordova with the Kennecott copper mines in the Wrangell Mountains, began in Cordova in 1908. The railroad reached Chitina about 1910 and McCarthy the following year. Chitina quickly became an important railroad junction town: passengers and freight bound for the Interior transferred from the train to coach at Chitina, heading west on the Chitina-Tonsina spur road to meet up with the government wagon road linking Valdez and Fairbanks.

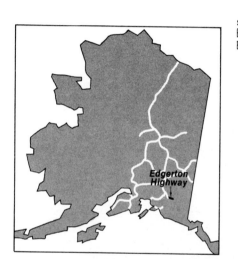

O.A. Nelson presents a visitor to Chitina with a "Skeleton Key." This photo appeared in the 1955 edition of The MILEPOST®, which described Chitina as having "a promising future, as the new highway from Cordova will connect here with the Edgerton Cut-off, to form a new link in the Alaska Highway system." A longtime Alaskan, O.A. Nelson, owned much of Chitina and had personally financed the building of two miles of road along the railroad grade at the Chitina end in his efforts to see the town linked with Cordova. (William Wallace photo, reprinted from The MILEPOST®)

East of Chitina, the railroad continued to McCarthy, a booming mining town just south of the rich Kennecott copper mines, and to the company town of Kennicott at the mine. (The town, river, and glacier are spelled Kennicott; the mines and mining company were misspelled Kennecott.)

The mine and railroad ceased operation in 1938, and the once-flourishing communities of Kennicott, Chitina, and McCarthy languished. In McCarthy and Kennicott, miners and merchants closed up their homes and shops and left. A proposed road from Cordova to Chitina over the old CR&NW railroad bed held some promise for Chitina. Residents remaining in McCarthy, where gold mining continued on a small scale, asked the Alaska Road Commission to extend the proposed highway to McCarthy.

The Copper River Highway from Cordova to Chitina was never completed, but the spur road from the Richardson Highway to Chitina was maintained. It was later named after Major Glen Edgerton of the Alaska Road Commission. The road from Chitina to McCarthy, however, was cut off by the Copper River. In their haste to complete the railway, the railroad's planned steel bridge across the Copper River — the so-called Chitina Bridge — was not built; instead a piling trestle was driven across the river, which had to be rebuilt each spring after breakup. Road access to McCarthy was reestablished in 1971 with the completion of the $3.5 million Copper River Bridge, a 1,378-foot steel span designed for year-round use.

Above — *Workers lay final section of railroad track at Kennecott mine in 1911, marking end of Copper River & Northwestern Railway.* (E.A. Hegg photo, Alaska Historical Library; reprinted from *The Copper Spike*)

Right — *Abandoned Kennecott mine near McCarthy. The mine operated from about 1910 until 1938, with copper production at its peak in quantity and value in 1916.* (Sharon Paul, staff)

Right — *Chitina in the early 1900s was an important stop on the Copper River & Northwestern: from here, passengers and freight bound for the Interior transferred to the Richardson Highway by coach.* (Ralph E. Mackay collection, reprinted from *The Copper Spike*)

Below — *Chitina (pronounced CHIT na) has a population of about 50 today. The small community is at the western boundary of Wrangell-Saint Elias National Park and Preserve.* (Sharon Paul, staff)

High-grade copper ore started it all, bringing mines, men, and the railroad to the Kennicott area.
(Sharon Paul, staff)

107

Kenny Lake on the Edgerton Cutoff. Scattered homesteads and farms are seen along the old and new Edgerton highways. (Sharon Paul, staff)

Today, the Edgerton Highway (Alaska Route 10) leads east to Chitina from Milepost 83 on the Richardson Highway. The first seven miles of this highway were completed in 1965, replacing the original or Old Edgerton Highway which meets the Richardson at Milepost 91. The old cutoff — still in use — is an 8-mile gravel road through the Kenny Lake homestead area. It intersects the newer highway 26 miles west of Chitina. Chitina, population about 50, consists of a few dozen clapboard houses, a post office, store, tire repair, flying service, bar, and gas station.

Beyond Chitina, the McCarthy Road continues east along the base of the Wrangell Mountains to McCarthy. For vehicles, the McCarthy Road ends about a mile west of McCarthy at the two forks of the Kennicott River. Here, two primitive hand-pulled cable trams provide the only means of crossing the river. About a dozen people live in McCarthy, which has a flying service, and two lodges. The Kennecott copper mines are four miles north of McCarthy. The mine, the town of McCarthy, and the McCarthy Road, along with hundreds of relics from the area's heyday, are located within the 12-million-acre Wrangell-Saint Elias National Park and Preserve.

Aerial view of University Range, Root and Kennicott glaciers in Wrangell-Saint Elias area. Town of Kennicott is just right of center. (George Herben, reprinted from *ALASKA GEOGRAPHIC*®)

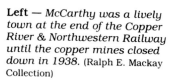

Left — *McCarthy was a lively town at the end of the Copper River & Northwestern Railway until the copper mines closed down in 1938.* (Ralph E. Mackay Collection)

Below — *McCarthy only has about a dozen residents today, but may get more visitors as more people discover Wrangell-Saint Elias National Park.* (Norman Nault)

Below — *A 63-mile dirt road east from Chitina follows old railroad bed to McCarthy. The steel-span bridge seen in distance was built in 1971.* (Sharon Paul, staff)

Kuskulana Bridge, called the "biggest thrill on the road to McCarthy" by motorists, crosses 238 feet above the Kuskulana River. The three-span steel railway bridge is at Mile 17 McCarthy Road. (Sharon Paul, staff)

Maintaining the McCarthy Road

By Sam Taylor
Reprinted from ALASKA® magazine

In April of 1977 I was dispatched as an equipment operator for the Chitina Maintenance Station of the Alaska Department of Transportation. Although we do 90% of our work on the new and old Edgerton Highways, we do spend some devoted days repairing and maintaining the McCarthy Road.

Driving the grader across the narrow Kuskulana Bridge is an eyes-on-the-road job. (Sam Taylor, reprinted from *ALASKA®* magazine)

In the winter we plow snow approximately 27 miles, digging out the Kotzina Bluffs, scraping ice on the Kuskulana Bridge and widening for pull-outs.

Approaching the Kuskulana Bridge with a grader, you slow to a stop, shift into low and inch your way across the 525-foot expanse. During the entire crossing I never take my eyes off the bridge, look over the edge or take a picture.

One morning a fellow worker crossed the bridge, scraping ice. Then from a distance I could see the ice crystals falling the 238-foot drop. With the rising sun in the background you couldn't have asked for a more beautiful daybreak.

During the preceding summer we pulled shoulder spreading material across the surface road. From previous experience we knew we had to be careful of railroad spikes puncturing the grader's tires. To prevent this we pulled a gas-powered magnet, hoping to pick up the countless spikes.

This procedure not only uncovered over 300 main spikes, it also produced some 20 smaller dated spikes. We also found a number of plates which held the rail to the tie and a car coupler which connected the cars together.

Completing our excursion to Mile 45, we headed for home, wet and tired. After crossing the Copper River Bridge and climbing the hill toward the dump, we came upon a disaster. During our five-day absence, the unpredictable Copper River had changed channels. It was cutting hard against the bank, sending the

dump and a 40-foot section of road a good 30 feet down the embankment. This left some 50 fishermen and McCarthy Road residents trapped.

Cutting a new road higher up the bank took us two weeks; then the trapped vehicles had to be towed through a foot of mud with the assistance of a state bulldozer.

During the summer months we usually spend between 7 and 10 days on the general upgrading of the road. On some occasions though, we've been called out for various emergencies, including removing a mud slide and replacing a washed-out culvert.

The McCarthy Road has been used for some 69 years. Whether traveling by horseback, railroad or automobile, people have always been impressed by its rugged beauty.

Mud slide removal like this at Mile 42 of the McCarthy Road is just one of the maintenance tasks. (Sam Taylor, reprinted from *ALASKA*® magazine)

TAYLOR HIGHWAY

The Taylor Highway turns off the Alaska Highway about 12 miles east of Tok at an intersection known as Tetlin Junction (it has also been called Dawson or Fortymile junction). A narrow, gravel summer road, the 161-mile Taylor Highway winds north along ridge tops and mountainsides, descending into the valley of the Fortymile River and ending at the community of Eagle on the Yukon River.

Construction of the Taylor began in 1946; by 1951, motorists were driving up the first 96 miles of the Taylor to Jack Wade Junction, where they connected with a 60-mile dirt road to Dawson City. The last 65 miles of the Taylor Highway into Eagle were completed in late 1953.

Today, thousands of tourists, miners, and locals use the Taylor Highway between spring breakup and winter freezeup (the road is closed from about October to April). It is still the shortest route (177 miles) for

On the Taylor Highway between Tetlin Junction and Chicken. The 161-mile road is gravel, open to vehicle traffic from about April to October. (Sharon Paul, staff)

Alaskans headed for Dawson City, and an alternate route for Alaska-bound drivers from the Yukon via the so-called Klondike Loop. The loop drive follows the Klondike Highway from its turnoff on the Alaska Highway just north of Whitehorse to Dawson City, then across the gravel Sixtymile Highway to the Taylor Highway and south on the Taylor back to the Alaska Highway. (The loop drive is about 504 miles, only 127 miles farther than driving the Alaska Highway between Whitehorse and Tetlin Junction.)

But many who turn up the Taylor Highway are bound for the old gold rush settlement of Eagle. The Taylor Highway roughly parallels part of the Valdez-to-Eagle trail first used during the Klondike gold rush and in succeeding years as a military road between Fort Liscum (now Dayville at

Ann Purdy, author of the book Tisha, *makes biscuits in the kitchen of her home near Chicken. (Sharon Paul, staff)*

115

Chicken (the cluster of buildings in photo at right) is a former mining camp, located at Milepost 67 on the Taylor Highway, with a population of 37 and a single business (pictured below). The origin of the name is uncertain. One story has it that the miners wanted to name the camp ptarmigan, but unable to spell it settled for chicken, the common name in the North for ptarmigan. Yet another story relates that the first prospectors found gold nuggets here the size of dried corn commonly fed to chickens. (Sharon Paul, staff)

Right — *U.S. Army's Eagle City Camp, established in 1899 at Eagle on the Yukon River. Fort Egbert was built the following year.* (Courtesy of R.N. De Armond, reprinted from *ALASKA GEOGRAPHIC*®)

Opposite — *Wet, fall day in Eagle, at the end of the Taylor Highway.* (Sharon Paul, staff)

116

Above — *Athabascan settlement of Eagle Village is three miles upstream from the city of Eagle by road. The village has a population of 54; Eagle city's population is 110.* (Sharon Paul, staff)

Right — *Eagle resident John Berg tells visitors about the restored grounds at Fort Egbert. The old Army post is located at the north end of town.* (Sharon Paul, staff)

Inside Eagle's turn-of-the-century federal courthouse, first presided over by Judge James Wickersham (his portrait is at far left on front wall). Eagle's district court encompassed 300,000 square miles; the court was moved to Fairbanks in 1903. (Sharon Paul, staff)

City hall of Eagle, Interior Alaska's first incorporated city. (Sharon Paul, staff)

Valdez) and Fort Egbert. A supply point for miners in the Fortymile area in the late 1800s, by 1898 Eagle's population was an estimated 1,700. In 1903, the town had a post office, a federal courthouse, a military fort, and was connected to the outside world by telegraph. It was from Eagle in December 1905 that Roald Amundsen telegraphed that he had discovered the Northwest Passage.

By 1910, the population of Eagle had dwindled to 178. The Klondike gold rush was long over, and strikes — in Fairbanks, in Nome, and elsewhere — had lured away local miners. Fort Egbert was abandoned in 1911. Eagle's population continued to decline over the years, down to 54 in 1930, but gold mining continued on a small scale in the area. (In May 1938, residents and inhabitants of the Fortymile Mining District unsuccessfully petitioned the Alaska Road Commission for construction of a road to connect the mining camps at Jack Wade and Chicken.)

With the completion of the Taylor Highway (Alaska Route 5) in 1953, access to this historic mining area was reestablished. The skyrocketing price of gold in the late 1970s has led to something of a modern-day gold rush taking place along the Taylor. High-pressure hoses, bulldozers and suction dredges have replaced the old gold dredges and sluice boxes that still lay abandoned beside the road. Old mine tailings are being reworked and old mining camps reopened.

The Taylor Highway is also an important link to one of Alaska's oldest highways, the Yukon River. The Yukon-Charley Rivers National Preserve can be reached by boat from Eagle, a fairly easy downstream route for canoes, kayaks, and rafts.

Eagle's monument to polar explorer Roald Amundsen, showing the Northwest Passage he discovered. In December 1905, Amundsen arrived in Eagle on foot, his ship Gjoa frozen in sea ice to the north, to telegraph news of his discovery to the outside world. (Sharon Paul, staff)

119

Right — *Modern-day small mining operation along the Fortymile River. With the high price for gold per troy ounce, streambeds in the Fortymile district are being reworked with renewed fervor.* (Harold Schetzle, reprinted from *ALASKA*® magazine)

Below — *Old dredge next to Taylor Highway, about 86 miles north of Tetlin Junction. The highway leads through Fortymile River country, an area that has been mined off and on for the past hundred years.* (David Skidmore)

Below — *Homestead alongside the Fortymile River on the Taylor Highway.* (Sharon Paul, staff)

Right — *The Yukon River flows past the community of Eagle. This great river cuts an almost 2,000-mile-long arcing course from its headwaters near Whitehorse to its mouth on Alaska's west coast. It was, and is, one of the North's most important navigable waterways.* (Sharon Paul, staff)

DENALI HIGHWAY

The Denali Highway winds 135 miles east and west along the southern flank of the Alaska Range, through a country of tundra meadows, scattered spruce and willow, and rivers that rise from glaciers in the high peaks to the north. For today's motorist, the Denali Highway is a scenic route to Denali National Park, connecting Paxson on the Richardson Highway with Cantwell on the George Parks Highway, just south of the park entrance. But in 1957, the just-completed Denali Highway was a pioneer road, the first and only road to Mount McKinley National Park (renamed Denali National Park in 1980).

Before the Denali Highway was built, Mount McKinley National Park was accessible only by rail. McKinley-bound travelers boarded the Alaska Railroad in Fairbanks or Anchorage for the three- to six-hour train ride to McKinley Park Station

Tundra meadows of Maclaren River valley are bathed in golden light. Hazy silhouettes beyond are the Clearwater Mountains. (Jon R. Nickles)

(now Denali Park Station). The 90-mile gravel road leading from the park entrance west to Kantishna was open to vehicles, and many visitors shipped their cars and trailers by rail to the park to make the tour by auto.

Construction of the Denali Highway began in 1949. With its completion in 1957, motorists could at last drive to the park: a 330-mile drive from Fairbanks, and some 425 miles from Anchorage. In 1971, the newly completed Anchorage-Fairbanks

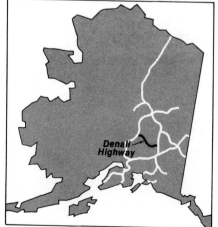

Above — *Willow ptarmigan, common in Central Alaska, in summer plumage.*
(Jon R. Nickles)

Right — *Wide-open tundra and spindly spruce of Denali country are flanked by the Alaska Range to the north. West Fork Glacier in distance terminates at the West Fork of the Susitna River.*
(Jon R. Nickles)

(George Parks) Highway established a more direct route to the park from the state's population centers.

The Denali Highway is a gravel road, open to traffic from about April to October. It is not a steep road, although it crosses Maclaren Summit, elevation 4,086 feet, the second highest highway pass in Alaska (Atigun Pass on the Dalton Highway, at 4,800 feet, is the highest). With the completion of the George Parks Highway in 1971, the Denali Highway was shortened by about 20 miles. The highway now ends at Cantwell, just west of the George Parks Highway junction; the road originally continued north past Carlo Creek and across the Nenana River to the national park entrance.

Alaska Route 8 was named for the mountain it led to: Denali, the Tanana Indian name for Mount McKinley, said to mean "the big one" or "high one."

Denali Highway bridges the Susitna River about 80 miles west of Paxson. One of the major rivers crossed by the highway, the Susitna flows southwest 260 miles to Cook Inlet. (Jon R. Nickles)

Right — *Grayling caught along the Denali Highway. Fishing for grayling and lake trout begins as soon as ice goes out on lakes and rivers, about mid-June.* (Jon R. Nickles)

Below — *Maclaren Glacier trends southwest from the Alaska Range to the head of Maclaren River.* (Jon R. Nickles)

Denali Highway follows shore of Teardrop Lake just west of Paxson. Highway pavement ends 10 miles west of here; the remaining 114 miles of highway are gravel.
(Jon R. Nickles)

Cloud-ringed Mount Drum looms above Glenn Highway on drive west. The 12,010-foot peak is in the Wrangell Mountains.
(Betty Johannsen)

128

GLENN HIGHWAY

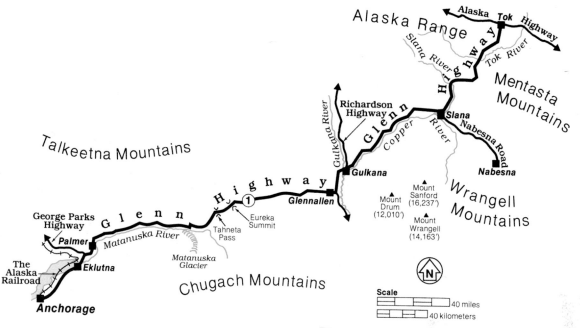

The principal access route from the Alaska Highway to Anchorage is the 328-mile Glenn Highway (Alaska Route 1). This modern paved highway, which puts Anchorage within a day's drive of Tok, follows a succession of early-day trails and wagon roads that became auto roads in the 1930s and 1940s. The highway has been rerouted and shortened over the years, but the country the road passes through, and some of the roadside businesses, have remained much as they were when the route opened in 1942.

The first 65 miles of the Glenn Highway out of Tok were known as the Slana-Tok Cutoff. This section of road was built by the U.S. Army Corps of Engineers in 1942 as a shortcut to Anchorage from the Alaska Highway. Slana, a small settlement at the confluence of the Copper and Slana rivers, is just south of the present-day Glenn Highway on the Nabesna Road.

The 45-mile-long Nabesna Road leads south to the former mining settlement of Nabesna and was part of an older transportation route, the Gulkana-Nabesna

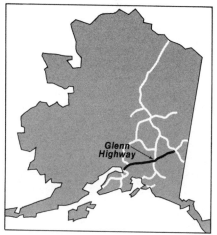

Narrow and bumpy Nabesna Road leads 45 miles south from Glenn Highway to the small settlement of Nabesna. (Sharon Paul, staff)

129

Road (opened for truck traffic in 1936), that linked the Richardson Highway with Nabesna.

Between Tok and the Richardson Highway junction at Gulkana, a distance of 125 miles, the Glenn Highway passes through a sparsely settled region north of the Mentasta and Wrangell mountains. For those traveling along this stretch of highway, there are ever-changing views of three peaks of the Wrangell Mountains: Mount Sanford, Mount Drum, and Mount Wrangell.

At the Gulkana River, the Glenn Highway joins the Richardson Highway and shares a common alignment with it for about 14 miles, until the Glenn turns west to the community of Glennallen. People living along the Glenn Highway, in small communities like Glennallen or on homesteads between towns, make their living in a variety of ways, from running roadside businesses to acting as guides and outfitters. Some of the lodges along the Glenn date back to the days when this was just a trail.

Construction of the Glenn Highway connecting the Richardson Highway with Palmer was begun in 1941 and completed — except for some final surfacing — in 1942. This 147-mile stretch of road was named after Captain E.F. Glenn, who made

Clockwise from above —
Raising and racing dogs, like this Alaska husky, is a pastime for many residents along the Glenn Highway.
(Sharon Paul, staff)

Gulkana River, just east of the Native village of Gulkana, marks the junction of the Glenn Highway with the Richardson Highway. Peak in background is Mount Sanford.
(Betty Johannsen)

Hart D Ranch, just off the Glenn Highway on Nabesna Road. The Slana post office is in the log building at left.
(Sharon Paul, staff)

Looking southeast on the Glenn Highway, just outside Glennallen, a view of three great peaks of the Wrangell Mountains: (from left) Mount Sanford, 16,237 feet; Mount Drum, 12,010 feet; and Mount Wrangell, 14,163 feet. (Sharon Paul, staff)

Community of Glennallen (population about 800), a trade and service center for the area, is located about midway between Tok and Anchorage on the Glenn Highway. (Sharon Paul, staff)

an early reconnaissance of the area for the U.S. Army in 1898. (The entire route from Tok to Anchorage is now generally referred to as the Glenn.)

West from Glennallen, the Glenn Highway crests 3,322-foot Eureka Summit, highest point on the highway. The summit view to the west takes in the Chugach Mountains, a 250-mile-long range of icy peaks that extends from Bering Glacier to Turnagain Arm, and the smaller Talkeetna Mountains to the northwest of the highway. From the summit, the Glenn Highway descends west through the Matanuska River valley to Palmer.

The great Matanuska Glacier, near the head of the Matanuska River in the Chugach Mountains, terminates just south of the Glenn Highway some 59 miles east of

Palmer. This 27-mile-long glacier is one of the few glaciers in Alaska accessible by automobile.

Following the Matanuska River west, the Glenn Highway enters Palmer, commercial center of the agriculturally rich Matanuska valley. The town of Palmer was established about 1916 as a railway station on the Matanuska Branch of The Alaska Railroad. (This railroad spur — and a tote road — extended east from Palmer to the coal mines at Jonesville, Buffalo, and Eska.) The Matanuska and Susitna river valleys, collectively known as the Mat-Su, were one of the earliest homestead areas in Alaska; an excellent system of roads served the farms and mines in the Mat-Su valley vicinity as early as the 1920s.

Eureka Summit, at 3,322-feet the highest point on the Glenn Highway, gives an unobstructed view south of the Chugach Mountains. (Sharon Paul, staff)

Left — *The Glenn Highway passes Leila Lake near 3,000-foot Tahneta Pass, 121 miles east of Anchorage.* (Sharon Paul, staff)

Below — *Cow moose photographed alongside the Glenn Highway. Alaska moose rank as the largest of their species, with males weighing up to 1,600 pounds, females to 1,200.* (Sharon Paul, staff)

Above — *Alaska's roadsides are brightened by a variety of wild flowers in spring and summer. This black-tipped groundsel was growing along the Nabesna Road.* (Sharon Paul, staff)

Overleaf — *Matanuska Glacier heads in the Chugach Mountains to the south. The glacier is accessible by a side road from the Glenn Highway, 102 miles east of Anchorage.* (Sharon Paul, staff)

Sharon Paul, staff

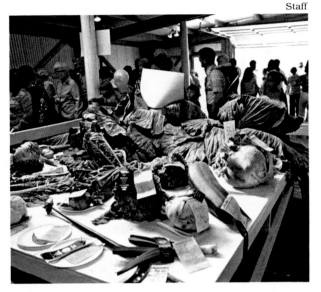

Staff

Kelly Wilson from Palmer heads out the Glenn Highway on a pack trip to eastern Canada. Horses sometimes seen along the highway belong to local packers. (Sharon Paul, staff)

The Matanuska Valley's 120-day growing season, warm temperatures, and 19 hours of daily sunlight produce sunflower in local garden (seen above) and prize-winning vegetables displayed at Palmer's Alaska State Fair at right.

Staff

Palmer, population 2,141, is located 42 miles north of Anchorage in the Matanuska Valley. Some 180 farm families from the Midwest settled in the valley during the 1930s under the auspices of the Alaska Rural Rehabilitation Corporation, a federal program. Modern farms, such as the one pictured at right, are found throughout the Matanuska Valley, where dairy farming and feed crops for cows are the dominant income source.

138

Betty Johannsen

From Palmer, it is only 42 miles to downtown Anchorage via the final leg of the Glenn Highway. This section of road has changed considerably since the highway was first logged in the 1949 edition of *The MILEPOST®*. Back then the Glenn bridged the Knik River several miles upstream from The Alaska Railroad crossing; today, the highway parallels the railroad crossing. A modern, divided freeway has replaced the old road into Anchorage, with freeway exits to old sites, like Eklutna Indian village, and to new housing developments that have become suburbs of Alaska's fastest-growing city, Anchorage.

The 1949 log of the Glenn Highway shows some of the changes that have taken place. Here is how the old highway log ended:

You are now approaching the military reserve surrounding Fort Richardson and must stop at the M.P. station just ahead. As you pass Fort Richardson you must stop again at the second M.P. station, on your left. It is only 4 miles from here into Anchorage. As you approach the city you pass the Municipal airport, Merrill Field, and must watch the stop signals as the approach to one runway traverses the highway.

The M.P. stations are gone, and the highway no longer crosses a runway (although Glenn Highway travelers can still watch small planes taking off and landing at Merrill Field, located just beside the highway). Anchorage has also changed, from a city of 15,000 in 1949, to a city of 180,000 today.

Anchorage lies on a broad peninsula on the upper shores of Cook Inlet, bordered on the east by the Chugach Mountains. Begun as a railroad construction camp in 1915, Anchorage today is a sprawling big city of skyscrapers and shopping centers, a center of commerce and distribution.

Glenn Highway outside Anchorage is a heavily traveled thoroughfare, and moose wandering across the road are a problem, especially in winter. (Sharon Paul, staff)

Right — *Brightly colored grave houses are painted in the family's traditional colors. These spirit houses are in the cemetery at Eklutna, an Indian village 26 miles north of Anchorage just off the Glenn Highway.* (Staff)

Below — *Glenn Highway approach to Anchorage has changed considerably over the years. The modern cloverleaf and straight stretch of freeway have replaced the old turnoffs and winding road.* (Third Eye Photography)

141

Looking over downtown Anchorage and beyond to the Chugach Mountains from the top of the Captain Cook Hotel on Fifth and K streets. Fifth Street connects with the Glenn Highway a few miles east of downtown.
(Dianne Hofbeck, staff)

143

GEORGE PARKS HIGHWAY

When the Anchorage-Fairbanks Highway opened in 1971, reactions among residents along the route ranged from regret at the influx of people and traffic ("no more running our dogs on the road," one woman said) to optimism about new business (a service station in Cantwell fixed 50 flat tires on opening day). When asked what difference the new highway would make, one resident replied laconically, "About four hours."

Prior to completion of the 323-mile Anchorage-Fairbanks Highway (it was renamed in 1975 after former territorial governor George Parks), travel between Anchorage, Fairbanks, and Mount McKinley National Park was either by road — a roundabout drive on three different highways — or via the more direct Alaska Railroad.

On clear days, 20,320-foot Mount McKinley is visible from the George Parks Highway. (Betty Johannsen)

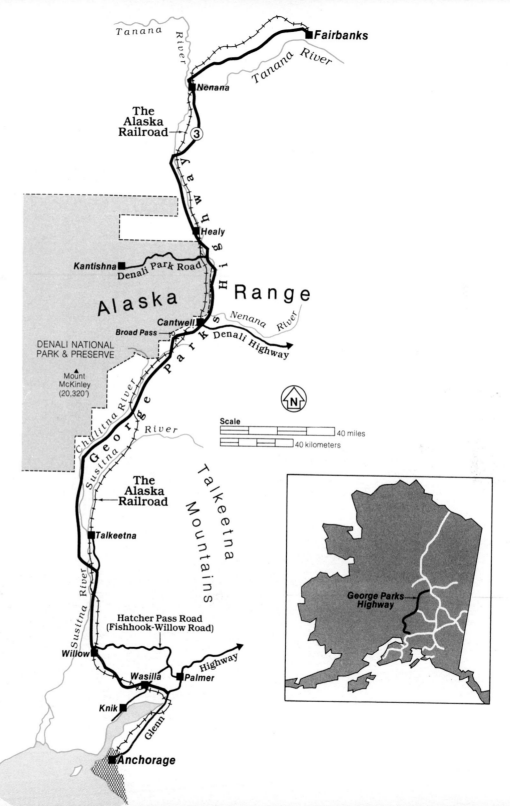

George Parks Highway curves along the Nenana River near the entrance to Denali National Park.
(Sharon Paul, staff)

Construction of the highway began in 1959. By 1966, Alaska Route 3 from the southern or Anchorage approach had been completed as far as the Susitna River bridge and a secondary road constructed to Talkeetna. The northern approach from Fairbanks followed the 60-mile Nenana Highway to the Tanana River ferry ($1.50 car and driver), and then beyond Nenana another 60 miles to within 7.5 miles of Mount McKinley National Park (renamed Denali National Park and Preserve in 1980). The Tanana River Bridge replaced the ferry at Nenana in 1967; it is one of more than 40 bridges on the highway. Estimated cost of the highway by the time it was completed in 1971 was $150 million. The 4.8 miles of road through the rugged Nenana Canyon cost $7.7 million to build.

Today, the George Parks Highway is a smooth, wide paved highway, maintained year-round. The steepest grade in the first 150 miles out of Anchorage is only 7.5 percent. From its junction with the Glenn Highway 35 miles northeast of Anchorage, the George Parks curves northward through the Susitna River valley, following the Chulitna River to 2,300-foot Broad Pass. Some 237 miles north of Anchorage, the highway reaches the entrance to Denali National Park and Preserve. From the park entrance it is a 121-mile drive north to Fairbanks.

The George Parks Highway roughly parallels the older railroad link between Anchorage and Fairbanks — The Alaska Railroad. Before the George Parks Highway was completed, The Alaska Railroad provided

Clockwise from above —
Clear summer day at Broad Pass (elevation 2,300 feet), a wide mountain valley some 155 miles south of Fairbanks surrounded by peaks of the Alaska Range.
(Sharon Paul, staff)

Looking for blueberries in early September at Broad Pass. (Staff)

George Parks Highway is kept open all year to traffic, although winter travelers are warned to check highway conditions before proceeding.
(Pete Martin)

the most direct route between the two major cities. The railroad was the only link to Mount McKinley park until the Denali Highway opened in 1957.

The Alaska Railroad began in 1912 with the appointment by Congress of a commission to study transportation problems in Alaska. The railway was to open up the agricultural lands and mineral resources of the Interior, connecting them with harbors on the southern coast of Alaska. The Alaska Engineering Commission surveyed possible railroad routes in 1914, and in April 1915, President Woodrow Wilson announced the selection of a route from Seward north 412 miles to the Tanana

Left — *The Alaska Railroad parallels the George Parks Highway between Anchorage and Fairbanks. Train trip between the two cities takes about ten hours, including a stop at Denali National Park station.* (Sharon Paul, staff)

Above — *Anchorage depot of The Alaska Railroad is a short walk from downtown.* (Staff)

River. Branch lines were extended east from Matanuska, a railroad station about six miles southwest of present-day Palmer, to Chickaloon and Sutton and the coal fields at Buffalo Mine, Jonesville, and Eska.

The main line was extended beyond the Tanana River to Fairbanks, with branch lines to the coal fields at Healy and north from Fairbanks (via the Tanana Valley Railroad's narrow-guage line) to the Chatanika mining district. The gold spike marking completion of the railroad was driven by President Warren G. Harding at Nenana on July 15, 1923. In 1930, the branch line to Chatanika was discontinued. The Matanuska branch lines to Sutton, Chickaloon, and the mines

Above — *President Warren G. Harding drives in the golden spike at Nenana on July 15, 1953, marking completion of The Alaska Railroad.*
(Courtesy of Marguerite Bone Wilcox, reprinted from *The ALASKA JOURNAL®*)

Left — *Riding in the "Speeder" is Mrs. Warren G. Harding on a trip up The Alaska Railroad in 1923.*
(Courtesy of Marguerite Bone Wilcox, reprinted from *The ALASKA JOURNAL®*)

149

Fall colors the landscape near Healy. A four-mile branch line of the Alaska Railroad connects coal mines near here with the main railway line.
(Third Eye Photography)

were discontinued between 1933 and 1970.

The Alaska Railroad continues to offer year-round passenger and freight service between Anchorage and Fairbanks.

Construction of the railroad in the early 1900s brought development to the country, from tent towns for the workers to railway stations. Some of those early stations, such as Talkeetna, Wasilla, and Nenana, became

fair-sized communities on the newer highway. A few railroad flagstops, like Lignite and Sunshine, were placenames which appeared on maps of the area for many years, but have since vanished. Other localities still bear the name given them by railroad builders. Montana Creek got its name as a railroad camp in 1919. Today, about 200 families live in the area around Milepost 96 Montana Creek, which was homesteaded in the late 1950s.

Clockwise from left — *Main Street of Talkeetna (population 264) is at the end of a 14.5-mile paved spur road off the George Parks Highway.* (Sharon Paul, staff)

Nenana, at the confluence of the Tanana and Nenana rivers, 54 miles south of Fairbanks, is an important transfer point from rail to river. A tug and barge fleet here carries supplies to villages along the Tanana and Yukon rivers in summer. (Tom Walker)

Honolulu Station on The Alaska Railroad line, approximately 174 miles north of Anchorage. (Dorothea Musgrave)

Wasilla, 42 miles north of Anchorage on the George Parks Highway, was a railway station on The Alaska Railroad in 1916. The town's main street is east of the highway. (Sharon Paul, staff)

Settlement along the George Parks Highway preceded both the highway and the railroad. Early reports show Tanaina Indian villages at the present-day sites of Talkeetna and Knik. In the early part of the century, gold, silver, and coal brought miners to Willow, Healy, and other settlements. In 1907, the Alaska Gold Quartz Mining Company staked claims in the Hatcher Pass area, where their Independence Mine operated until the 1940s. Independence Mine is now a state historical park; it can be reached via the old Fishhook-Willow (Hatcher Pass) Road off the George Parks Highway.

But the railroad accelerated settlement of this country, particularly in the Susitna and Matanuska valleys, where trainloads of homesteaders arrived in the 1930s.

The populations of communities along the George Parks Highway have increased considerably since the highway opened, and the number of highway services — campgrounds, lodges, restaurants, gas stations, and gift shops — has naturally grown since 1971. The growth of nearby Anchorage has helped increase development in the Susitna and Matanuska valleys. But for all the growth along the highway, the George Parks still crosses miles and miles of rugged, untouched country.

Opposite — *Independence Mine State Historical Park, about 37 miles east of the highway on Hatcher Pass Road, includes mining machinery and several wood frame buildings used when the mine operated between 1907 and 1948.* (Staff)

Left — *An old mining road, the Hatcher Pass Road (also called the Fishhook-Willow Road) is steep, narrow, winding, and not recommended for winter travel.* (Third Eye Photography)

153

Above — *Willow, population 139, grew rapidly after the area was designated as the proposed new Alaska capital site in 1976, but Alaska voters turned down the move in 1982.* (Sharon Paul, staff)

Below — *Much real estate development has been taking place along the highway between Willow and Anchorage.* (Sharon Paul, staff)

Above — *Trees turn to fall colors as early as August in Alaska.* (Sharon Paul, staff)

Right — *Hurricane Gulch highway bridge, 174 miles north of Anchorage, is one of more than 40 bridges on the George Parks. The highway bridge crosses 260 feet above Hurricane Creek; nearby Hurricane Gulch railroad bridge crosses 296 feet above the creek.* (Sharon Paul, staff)

154

The Road to Mount McKinley

When the George Parks Highway opened in 1971, rangers at Mount McKinley National Park felt some trepidation at the prospect of overflow crowds of visitors from Anchorage and Fairbanks. The new highway would replace the Denali Highway route to the park, saving Anchorage drivers some 180 miles, and Fairbanks drivers about 200 miles. If visitor statistics are any indication, their fears were realized: visitors to the park in 1971 numbered 58,342; in 1972, the number of visitors increased to 306,017. (The number of visitors to the park in recent years has averaged about 500,000.)

There is only one road in the

Profile of bull moose shows the bell (a skin tab hanging from lower neck) and great drooping nose of the species that makes a moose attractive only to another moose.
(Tom Walker)

Base of Mount McKinley
viewed from the park road
near Stony Hill. The 90-mile
gravel road through Denali
National Park comes within
27 miles of the summit of
Mount McKinley.
(Sharon Paul, staff)

Fishing for lake trout at
Wonder Lake, 84 miles west of
the park entrance near the
end of the park road. The
park's silted glacial rivers and
small lakes support small
numbers of grayling, Dolly
Varden, and lake trout.
(John Johnson)

5.6-million-acre Denali National Park and Preserve (Mount McKinley National Park was renamed and enlarged in 1980 with the passage of the Alaska lands bill). Construction of the park road was initiated in 1922 as a cooperative project between the Alaska Road Commission and Park Service. Begun in 1922, five years after Mount McKinley National Park was created, the road was completed in 1940. It leads west 90 miles from the park entrance on the George Parks Highway to the former mining settlement of Kantishna. It is a wilderness road: a narrow, gravel track across the alpine tundra on the north flank of the Alaska Range. Along the road visitors can see all of the park's wildlife: grizzly bear, moose, caribou, Dall sheep, beaver, arctic hare, and other small mammals. From Eielson Visitor Center, Milepost 66 on the park road, one gets the best view of the park's most famous attraction, 20,320-foot Mount McKinley.

Until the Denali Highway opened in 1957, the park was accessible only by railroad. Visitors shipped their cars and trailers to the park via The Alaska Railroad from Anchorage or Fairbanks, unloaded at McKinley (now Denali) Park Station, and drove out the park road.

After completion of the George Parks Highway, the National Park Service instituted a controlled-access system for park road use, restricting the number of vehicles using the park road. Still in effect today, private vehicle traffic on the park road beyond the Savage River bridge (Milepost 14.5) is restricted to registered campers; motorists with camping permits may drive only to their campsites.

The Park Service operates a free shuttle bus service in summer between Riley Creek visitor center, near the park entrance, and Wonder Lake. The buses pick up and drop off passengers at any point along the park road. Round trip to Eielson visitor center takes about eight hours.

Camp Denali, the cluster of cabins in background, was begun by Celia Hunter and Ginny Wood in the 1950s, patterned after European-style lodges they had seen in the Swiss Alps. Camp Denali is located near Kantishna at the end of the park road. (Staff)

Left — *Broad valley of the Toklat River near Polychrome Pass. There are few established trails in the park, but there is plenty of open terrain for cross-country hiking.* (Steve Owlett)

Right — *Free shuttle bus, operated by National Park Service, stops at Eielson Visitor Center daily in summer on its eight-hour round trip from the park entrance. Eielson offers the best view of Mount McKinley from the park road.* (Sharon Paul, staff)

159

Sharon Paul, staff

Third Eye Photography

Turnagain Pass in summer (upper) and in winter (right). Seward Highway traverses this mountain pass some 57 miles south of Anchorage. Glacier-fed streams lace meadows of wild flowers in summer; in winter, this is a favorite area for cross-country skiers.

160

KENAI PENINSULA HIGHWAYS

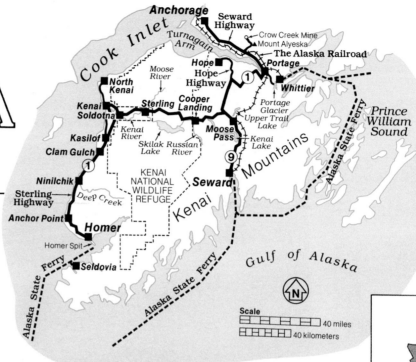

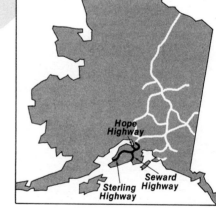

With the completion in 1951 of the so-called Turnagain Highway from Anchorage south around Turnagain Arm to Turnagain Pass, the Kenai highway system was finally linked by road to Anchorage and the rest of Alaska. Today, the Kenai Peninsula highway system consists of the Seward Highway (Alaska Routes 1 and 9); the Sterling Highway; and the Hope Highway. The Alaska Railroad and the state's southwestern ferry system link Kenai Peninsula ports to Prince William Sound.

Paralleling The Alaska Railroad from Anchorage around Turnagain Arm, the first 50 miles of the 127-mile Seward Highway were the last to be constructed. This final link follows the north shore of Turnagain Arm, a scenic stretch of road blasted from solid rock, and junctions with the Alyeska and Crow Creek access roads, the Portage Glacier access road, and the railroad shuttle to Whittier. Mount Alyeska, three miles from

Frozen cascade of ice on the Seward Highway. In summer, dozens of small waterfalls tumble down the brushy slopes along the highway.
(Pete Martin)

161

Potter Marsh (right), 10 miles south of Anchorage along the Seward Highway, is a nesting ground for a variety of bird life, like the Canada geese pictured below, and a favorite spot for local bird-watchers.

Jon R. Nickles

Third Eye Photography

the Seward Highway, is Alaska's largest ski resort. Crow Creek, one of the Kenai's early gold mines, is a national historic site located just north of Alyeska on a rough single-lane road. Portage Glacier, five miles east of the Seward Highway, was on the portage route used by early travelers between Passage Canal on Prince William Sound and Turnagain Arm. The turnoff for Portage Glacier access road is just south of The Alaska Railroad's Whittier Cutoff.

The railroad spur to Whittier was built by the Army Corps of Engineers during World War II, a measure to safeguard military supplies by shortening the distance from tidewater to Anchorage and giving the railroad two ports, Whittier and Seward. The Whittier Cutoff, from Portage station on the main railway line to Whittier on Passage Canal, still provides the only access to Whittier. The Alaska Railroad offers passenger service south from Anchorage to

Seward Highway curves around Turnagain Arm, paralleling the Alaska Railroad. This section of road was the final link between Anchorage and the Kenai Peninsula.
(Third Eye Photography)

Portage, with summer shuttle service for passengers and vehicles between Portage and Whittier. (At Whittier, the state ferry and private cruise boats take passengers across Prince William Sound, past the magnificent Columbia Glacier, to Valdez.) Freight service only is available to Seward.

About 70 miles south of Anchorage, the Seward Highway meets the 17-mile paved Hope Highway, part of the older route that connected the port of Seward with the gold mining settlements in the Hope-Sunrise district near Turnagain Arm and Resurrection Creek.

The Kenai's gold rush was modest compared to the great Klondike gold rush. The biggest strikes were in the area of Sunrise (a now vanished mining town) and Hope. Gold mining — and some quartz mining — continued from the 1890s through the 1930s at places such as Hope, Sunrise, Moose Pass, and Crow Creek. Rough trails,

Opposite — Narrow, winding stretch of Seward Highway along Turnagain Arm was blasted out of solid rock of the Chugach Mountains.
(Jon R. Nickles)

Left — *View of Portage Glacier and icebergs from the glacier floating in Portage Lake. Located in Chugach National Forest, there are a visitor center, campgrounds, and scheduled hikes and nature programs at Portage Glacier*
(Jon R. Nickles)

Above — *One of a dozen historic buildings at Crow Creek Mine, an early lode mine on the Kenai Peninsula. Listed on the National Register of Historic Sites, the mining camp is about five miles east of the Seward Highway.* (Sharon Paul, staff)

165

Alaska state ferry at Whittier carries passengers and vehicles across Prince William Sound to Valdez. (Third Eye Photography)

Vehicles on The Alaska Railroad shuttle train from Portage to Whittier. The train ride, which takes about 35 minutes, is offered several times daily in summer. There is also once-a-day service between Anchorage and Whittier. (Tom Walker)

Left — *Star attraction of Prince William Sound cruise is Columbia Glacier, one of the largest and most magnificent of Alaska's tidewater glaciers. The glacier is 41 miles long, and its terminus is 2.5 miles wide.* (Dianne Hofbeck, staff)

Below — *Close-up look at the face of Columbia Glacier from the Vince Peede, operated by Stan Stephens Charters. Charter operators in Whittier and Valdez offer a variety of tours across Prince William Sound.* (Sharon Paul, staff)

Above — *Mining settlement of Hope on Resurrection Creek, in 1948.* (Mary J. Barry, reprinted from *Mining on the Kenai Peninsula*)

Below — *Hope today, population 90, at the end of the Hope Highway on Turnagain Arm.* (Sharon Paul, staff)

then wagon roads, connected the settlements. The Bureau of Public Roads upgraded the Seward to Hope road to automobile standards in the 1920s. This early road ran from Seward to the south shore of Kenai Lake and a 10-mile gap (called the missing link); from Moose Pass the road continued uninterrupted to Hope.

From the Hope turnoff, today's Seward Highway heads south past Summit Lake to intersect with the Sterling Highway to Homer. From this junction it is 37 miles south to Seward on Resurrection Bay and the Gulf of Alaska, and 138 miles west on the Sterling Highway to Homer on Cook Inlet.

Opened in 1950, the Sterling Highway connected the small communities and scattered homesteads on the west coast of the Kenai Peninsula with the Seward

Decaying cabin along Resurrection Creek near Hope. Gold seekers worked Resurrection Creek and its tributary streams in the late 1800s and early 1900s. Today, the 38-mile Resurrection Pass trail follows this creek from Hope south to the Sterling Highway. (Sharon Paul, staff)

Seward, at the end of the Seward Highway, is nestled between high mountain ranges and Resurrection Bay. This community of 1,800 people depends on lumber and fisheries, and is also the terminus of the Alaska Railroad. (Chlaus Lotscher)

Glassy surface of Upper Summit Lake, 82 miles south of Anchorage, reflects surrounding hills. There is a Forest Service campground on the shore of this lake.
(Staff)

Kenai River, one of the Kenai Peninsula's best fishing streams, heads at Kenai Lake and flows west 75 miles to Cook Inlet. (Sharon Paul, staff)

171

A moose grazing along the Sterling Highway. A large part of Kenai National Wildlife Refuge was originally Kenai National Moose Range, set aside in 1941 to protect the habitat. (Sharon Paul, staff)

The Sterling Highway cuts across part of the nearly 2-million-acre Kenai National Wildlife Refuge. (Betty Johannsen)

Highway on the east side by extending an older branch road that reached a short distance past Cooper Landing.

From its junction with the Seward Highway west to Cook Inlet, the Sterling Highway (named in honor of Hawley Sterling, ARC engineer) cuts through the heart of the magnificent Kenai Peninsula. This is prime fishing country, and the highway provides access to many of the great fishing streams and lakes of the Kenai. This section of highway also traverses the Kenai National Wildlife Refuge, an almost 2-million-acre wilderness that is home to moose and Dall sheep, and destination for Anchorage residents who drive down to camp, canoe, and fish.

The Sterling Highway also provides access to the resource-rich Cook Inlet, a region that has experienced a steady influx of settlers since the 1700s. From north of Kenai south to Homer, the highway follows the west shore of Cook Inlet; side roads and footpaths branch off the highway, down to beaches for clamming, camping, and surf-fishing, and to the mouths of rivers where record-breaking salmon are caught.

Indian fishing villages, then Russian settlements, dotted the west coast of the Kenai Peninsula in the 1700s. The Russians established their first permanent settlement on mainland Alaska at Kasilof (then named St. George) and left behind signs of their occupation at Kenai and Ninilchik.

In the late 1800s, miners worked the gold placers on the beaches of Cook Inlet and the first oil claims were staked. The gold panned

Left — *Privately operated ferry takes fishermen across the Kenai River to mouth of Russian River. The Kenai-Russian River recreation area, a favorite with fishermen during salmon season, is located 108 miles from Anchorage on the Sterling Highway.* (Sharon Paul, staff)

Above — *Fishing on the Moose River. This river, which flows into the Kenai River, has a big summer run of reds and a run of silver salmon into October.* (Sharon Paul, staff)

173

Left — *Old village of Ninilchik, 38 miles north of Homer, was settled around the turn of the century by Creoles, Russians, Aleuts, and Indians. This historic village is at the mouth of Ninilchik River on Cook Inlet.* (Sharon Paul, staff)

Right — *Russian church at Kenai is a reminder of the Kenai Peninsula's Russian past. Kenai, 11 miles north of the Sterling Highway at the mouth of the Kenai River, was the second permanent settlement established by the Russians on mainland Alaska; Kasilof was the first.* (Sharon Paul, staff)

Below — *Overlooking the historic village of Ninilchik, this Russian Orthodox church was built in the early 1900s; the cemetery here is still in use.* (Staff)

Left — *A fisherman works at his nets on a beach near Clam Gulch, 55 miles north of Homer. Cook Inlet beaches along the Sterling Highway are busy with clam diggers, fishermen, and campers from early spring into fall.* (Sharon Paul, staff)

Above — *Mount Iliamna dominates the skyline of the Alaska Peninsula across Cook Inlet from the Sterling Highway. This view is from Deep Creek wayside, 36 miles north of Homer, a favorite area for surf fishing.* (Sharon Paul, staff)

Below — *Howard Maw from Oregon shows off the king salmon he caught at Deep Creek, one of the best salt-water king salmon fishing areas on the Kenai.* (Sharon Paul, staff)

out, but the oil did not. In 1957, Atlantic Richfield drilled the first producing oil well on the Kenai near Swanson River. A large gas field was later discovered at Kalifonsky Beach, and the first gas offshore location in Cook Inlet was found in 1962. Today, there are more than a dozen production platforms in Cook Inlet.

Approaching Homer on the Sterling Highway, motorists get their first glimpse of the narrow, gravel Homer Spit and beyond it, Kachemak Bay. At the turn of the century, coal mining was under way in the Kachemak Bay area. The name Kachemak, said to mean "smokey bay" in Aleut, is supposed to have come from the smoldering coal seams on the north shore of the bay. (Lumps of coal found on the beach — eroded from the cliffs above — provide fuel for local residents.)

The Sterling Highway ends in downtown Homer, a community of 2,200, homesteaded in the early 1920s. A picturesque town, backed by the Kenai Mountains, one of Homer's busiest streets is the Homer Spit road. Kachemak Bay and Cook Inlet are rich in marine life, keeping Homer Spit's fishing piers, seafood plants, charter operators, and small boat harbor busy with hauls of halibut, king, Dungeness, and tanner crab.

Across the bay from Homer is the small fishing community of Seldovia, accessible by state ferry.

Drilling rig, temporarily anchored at Kachemak Bay, under a September moon. There are more than a dozen offshore drilling platforms in Cook Inlet. An underwater pipeline links platforms to onshore facilities at Kenai and other sites. (Staff)

Petrochemical development at Port Nikishki, north of Kenai. The industrial complex in this area is part of the burgeoning oil development in Cook Inlet. (Staff)

177

Left — Sterling Highway winds down west shore of Cook Inlet and ends at Homer, about 226 miles from Anchorage. (Sharon Paul, staff)

Below — Homer Spit juts out into Kachemak Bay beneath the awesome peaks of the Kenai Mountains.
(Jon R. Nickles)

Businesses line the road on narrow Homer Spit, Homer's busiest thoroughfare.
(Tom Walker)

178

Above — *Crab can be purchased right off the boat from local fishermen at Homer.* (Sharon Paul, staff)

Right — *Homer small boat harbor on a foggy September morning.* (Staff)

Left — *Kachemak Bay and Cook Inlet are two of Alaska's most popular spots for halibut fishing, and displays of the big fish for sale are a common sight in Homer.*
(Sharon Paul, staff)

Below — *Seldovia, a community of less than 500 people, is across Kachemak Bay from Homer. There is no road access to this small fishing community; the state ferry system provides transportation.*
(Sharon Paul, staff)

ELLIOTT HIGHWAY

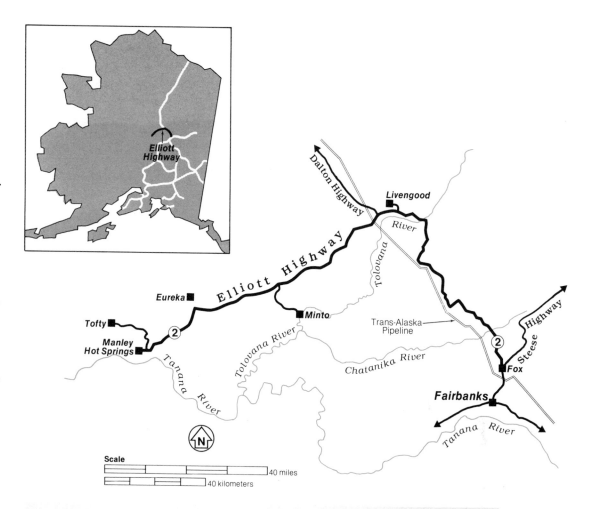

The Elliott Highway, connecting Fox and Manley Hot Springs, had its beginnings in 1906 as a summer wagon road from the mining camp of Fox to Olnes, a mining camp and railroad station on the Tanana Valley Railroad. In 1915, a sled road from Olnes to Livengood was built. Gold had been discovered at Livengood the year before and by 1915 a lively mining camp — named after Jay Livengood, one of the gold discoverers — had grown up around the claim. Some 50 miles southwest of Livengood, sled roads and wagon roads connected the mining camps at Eureka (established in 1899), Tofty (established in 1908), and Hot Springs. Homesteaded in 1902, Hot Springs (renamed Manley Hot Springs in 1957) had a resort hotel and a population of 101 in 1910.

By 1936, the 71-mile Olnes-Livengood

Left — *Elliott Highway travels the ridges and rolling hills of the Yukon-Tanana highlands between Fox and Manley Hot Springs.* (Sharon Paul, staff)

Right — *A wagon train waits at Fox Station on the Tanana Valley Railroad, circa 1910.* (Courtesy of Terrence Cole, reprinted from *E.T. Barnette*)

Livengood, 71 miles north of Fox on the Elliott Highway, has had a checkered past: a lively mining camp in the early 1900s, then a ghost town for some 20 years, and in the 1970s a construction camp for the trans-Alaska pipeline. A mining corporation is working the area now. (Sharon Paul, staff)

Road (renamed the Elliott Highway that year) was passable for automobiles for the first 40 miles. The highway was completed to Manley Hot Springs in 1959, but by that time most of the old mining camps along the route were ghost towns. Fox, at the junction with the Steese, had a general store and coffee shop. In the 1963 edition of The MILEPOST®, Livengood advertised an inn with a "ghost town atmosphere." Manley Hot Springs was a quiet settlement with a trading post, roadhouse, and airfield. Arrangements could be made with the owner of the hot springs to take a dip in the springs. Eureka, Tofty, and Olnes were abandoned.

Construction of the trans-Alaska pipeline and the rising price of gold helped revitalize

Gauzy, white Alaska cotton along the Elliott Highway (left). Cotton grass makes a lasting bouquet if picked before the seeds ripen.

Wild flowers to watch for in spring along the Elliott Highway include arnica (above) and wild iris (below). (All photos by Sharon Paul, staff)

185

Manley residents come to work their huge vegetable garden. There are some enthusiastic gardeners in Manley Hot Springs and the result are some outstanding displays of vegetables and berries in summer.
(Sharon Paul, staff)

Clockwise from above — *Caviar and lox produced by Interior Fisheries at Manley Hot Springs.*
(Sharon Paul, staff)

Cache at Manley Hot Springs. These storage units, built to be inaccessible to animals, have long been used by trappers and homesteaders as a primitive freezer in winter and for storage in summer.
(Sharon Paul, staff)

Cabbage is a common garden crop and a major farm crop in Alaska. (Sharon Paul, staff)

some of the communities along the Elliott in the 1970s.

The trans-Alaska pipeline parallels the Elliott Highway from the highway's junction with the Dalton Highway (formerly the North Slope Haul Road) at Milepost 73.5 south to Fox. Abandoned buildings and trailers still stand near Livengood where a pipeline construction camp was located.

Active mining is once again under way at Livengood, Eureka, and Tofty.

Manley Hot Springs remains a pocket of pioneer Alaska, still a quiet settlement with a trading post, roadhouse, and airfield. The resort hotel is gone and the hot springs are not open to the public. The community of 61 people receives quite a bit of river traffic on the Tanana and air traffic from Fairbanks.

From its completion in 1959 until the late 1970s, the 152-mile Elliott Highway (Alaska Route 2) was known as the "Road to Nome." The proposed route was to continue west from Manley Hot Springs to Nome, and the subtitle "The Road to Nome — Completed to Manley Hot Springs" appeared under the Elliott Highway heading in editions of *The MILEPOST®* until 1978, when it was dropped. The idea for a road to Nome has not been dropped (particularly by Nome residents), but the probability of extending the Elliott almost 500 miles west to the Seward Peninsula is remote.

Rolling stretch of the Elliott Highway on the way into Manley Hot Springs. The last 42 miles of the highway are closed during winter. (Sharon Paul, staff)

189

STEESE HIGHWAY

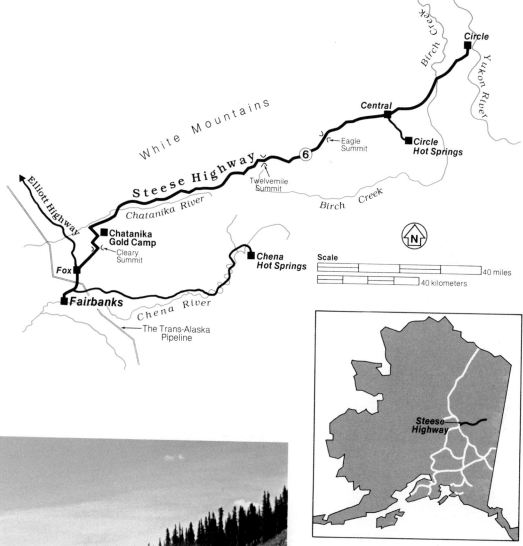

The Steese Highway, linking Fairbanks with Circle City on the Yukon, is one of Alaska's oldest roads. Like so many other Alaska roads, it began at the turn of the century as a trail to gold-bearing hills and streams and was eventually widened and upgraded to a freight road for miners. Today, the Steese is a 162-mile wide, mostly gravel, road (the first 44 miles are paved), that leads northeast to the communities of Central and Circle, with spur roads to Chena Hot Springs and Circle Hot Springs.

Gold mining along what is now the Steese Highway started as early as 1894 up in Circle City, where gold production was exceeding a million dollars annually two years before the Klondike gold rush. In 1902, Felix Pedro discovered gold on Pedro Creek (near the present-day location of Milepost 17), starting the rush that founded Fairbanks and brought miners to the Chatanika River,

Expansive view of the tundra-covered hills surrounding the Steese Highway near Twelvemile Summit, approximately 86 miles northeast of Fairbanks. (Sharon Paul, staff)

A truck kicks up the dust at Eagle Summit, elevation 3,624 feet, the third and highest summit on the Steese Highway. (Sharon Paul, staff)

Birch Creek, Mammoth Creek and other streams.

The mining settlement of Chatanika (Milepost 27.9) was established about 1904, and by 1907 the gold camp was connected to Fairbanks by the Tanana Valley Railroad. A road to connect Fairbanks, Chatanika, and Circle seemed a logical extension of the Richardson Highway which connected Valdez and Fairbanks. In 1922, residents of Circle Mining District, "for the past 28 years . . . a continuous producer of gold," petitioned the Alaska Road Commission to hurry completion of the Chatanika-Circle Road. By 1926, two-thirds of the road was completed, with automobile traffic possible for 62 miles out of Fairbanks (or 32 miles beyond Chatanika) and some 50 miles at the Circle end passable for wagon traffic in summer. The Fairbanks to Circle road was finally completed in 1929 and Alaska Route 6 was named after the man who supervised the project, General James G. Steese of the Alaska Road Commission.

In the years following completion of the Steese Highway, the price of gold — and the population of the communities along the road — fluctuated. The log of the Steese Highway in the 1949 edition of *The MILEPOST*® helps explain the situation:

The highway passes the former gold camp of old Chatanika at mile 28, and reaches the site of the most recent placer operations at Chatanika.

(At Milepost 29). Chatanika,

Above — *Rusting gold pan and shovel unearthed by a modern mining operation. The old pipe is still used to carry water for a hydraulic mining operation nearby.*
(Kris Valencia, staff)

Below — *Longtime miner Walter Roman at his mining camp northeast of Fairbanks. Walter takes out about 100 ounces of gold in a season and has also unearthed from the permafrost a complete prehistoric buffalo, which scientists are now studying.*
(Kris Valencia, staff)

Left — *Gold dredge near Chatanika Camp, silent since the boom days ended in the early 1900s, is surrounded by old tailings, the gravel and boulders of upended stream beds worked many years ago.*
(Sharon Paul, staff)

Right — *This large pipe is a section of the Davidson Ditch, a system of ditches and inverted siphons built in 1925 by the Fairbanks Exploration Company. The pipeline was capable of carrying more than 56,000 gallons of water per minute, which was used to float gold dredges.*
(Sharon Paul, staff)

Amateur gold panners try their luck in a stream near Pedro monument, about 17 miles north of Fairbanks. Many of the streams along the Steese are already staked and no trespassing is allowed. (Sharon Paul, staff)

headquarters town of a large gold-dredging operation. It will be apparent that there is very little activity in Alaskan gold mining at present. After the enforced shutdown during the war, protracted shipping strikes, and the tremendously increased costs of equipment and labor made it impractical for resumption of mining on the prewar scale. Gold, selling at the fixed price of $35.00 per troy ounce, yielded a healthy profit on the basis of prewar operating costs, but does so no longer. Until the price of gold is advanced to a suitable bracket in the postwar inflationary scale, the situation in the industry is unlikely to change in Alaska.

The price of gold did go up, starting in the 1970s and peaking at nearly $1,000 per troy

Above — *Chatanika Gold Camp, now a restaurant, was built by Fairbanks Exploration Company in the early 1900s to support gold dredging operations in the valley.* (Sharon Paul, staff)

Right — *Old tailings and new cuts mark many of the streams along the Steese Highway. This large mining operation is near Eagle Summit.* (Sharon Paul, staff)

194

Chatanika River valley in August when the leaves start to turn. This meandering river is a favorite with canoeists. (Kris Valencia, staff)

Right — *Community of Central has a population of about 100 in winter, but it jumps to 700 in summer when the miners arrive.*
(Sharon Paul, staff)

Below — *Circle City on the Yukon, one of Alaska's earliest mining settlements, about 1906. Early traders and prospectors named the town Circle, wrongly assuming it was on the Arctic Circle, which is about 50 miles north.*
(Courtesy of R.N. De Armond, reprinted from *ALASKA GEOGRAPHIC®*)

ounce by 1980. Chatanika gold camp is now a restaurant, but there are renewed gold mining operations elsewhere along the Steese Highway, at Birch Creek and in the surrounding hills. Central, at Milepost 127.5, has a population of 100 in winter, but it swells to 700 in summer with the influx of miners.

Circle, the turn-of-the-century boom town, at the end of the Steese, was described in the 1949 edition of *The MILEPOST®* as ''nearly deserted, except for some Indian families, a school for natives, and the well-stocked store of the Northern Commercial Co.'' Today, Circle's population is about 100 and it still has a well-stocked trading post, in addition to dozens of sod-roofed log homes, a campground, airstrip, and charter fishing and flightseeing tours.

Camping, hiking, fishing, and canoeing along the Steese Highway are within an hour's drive of Fairbanks. Chena Hot Springs, an hour's drive from Fairbanks via the Steese Highway and Chena Hot Springs Road, and Circle Hot Springs, eight miles from Central, offer modern travelers the same amenities that drew early-day miners — a soak in the steaming waters.

The Steese Highway is open to Circle from mid-May to October; the road is not maintained in winter. The 44-mile paved portion is easy driving and the remaining 118 miles of gravel ranges from wide, straight, top-of-the-world stretches across the tundra, to narrower, winding sections of country road following birch and willow-covered riverbanks.

Right — *Circle City sign marks the end of the Steese Highway. The sign is at the Circle campground on the Yukon River, a channel of which is visible in the distance. During spring breakup on the river, ice jams sometimes cause flooding: in 1979, the Yukon rose to the bottom of this welcome sign.* (Sharon Paul, staff)

Below — *Residential Circle today is a neat collection of log homes and small cabins, many of them sod-roofed.* (Kris Valencia, staff)

197

Circle Hot Springs Road (right) leads eight miles south of Central to Circle Hot Springs resort (below). The old hotel there has been refurbished and an Olympic-sized hot springs pool has replaced the tent bathhouses once used by miners. (Both photos by Sharon Paul, staff)

Left — *Mineral hot springs at Chena Hot Springs resort were first reported in 1907 by U.S. Geological Survey field teams.* (Sharon Paul, staff)

Below — *Fishing on the Chena River, just off Chena Hot Springs Road. The 57-mile paved road provides access to the river, which is within the Chena River state recreation area. Largely undeveloped, the state has provided two camping areas and several turnouts along the river.* (Sharon Paul, staff)

DALTON HIGHWAY

The Dalton Highway is Alaska's newest highway. Built in 1974 as part of the trans-Alaska pipeline project, the 416-mile North Slope Haul Road — as it was formerly known — was turned over to the State of Alaska in 1978 and renamed the Dalton Highway.

Construction of the haul road began in April 1974, and was completed in 154 days. Designed as a service road for pipeline trucks and equipment, the 28-foot-wide gravel road connects Prudhoe Bay with the Elliott Highway. Its construction required some 25 million cubic yards of gravel and some sections of road were underlain with thick sheets of plastic foam insulation to prevent thawing of the permafrost and the subsequent breakdown of the highway. It is a very rough road (even truckers complain) and not recommended for passenger vehicles.

Dalton Highway, still referred to by many as the North Slope Haul Road or just Haul Road, was built in 1974 as a service road for the trans-Alaska oil pipeline. It was named for James Dalton, son of Jack Dalton (the man who blazed the Dalton Trail. (Sharon Paul, staff)

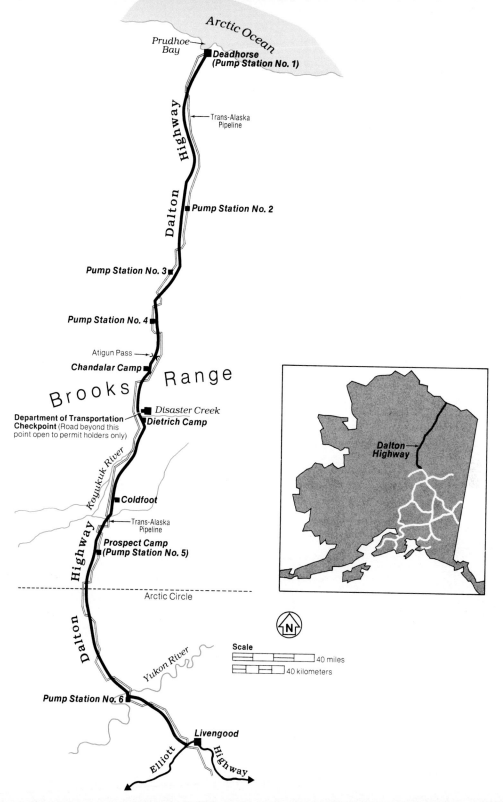

IMPORTANT ROAD INFORMATION
STEEP GRADES. WINDING ROAD.
DRIFTING SNOW. POOR VISIBILITY.
DELAYS DUE TO HEAVY EQUIPMENT.
HELL OF ALL KINDS
WIDE LOADS MAY BE EXPECTED

NEXT 56 MILES

Road conditions on the Dalton are extremely poor, as this sign at the start of the highway suggests.
(Sharon Paul, staff)

The haul road was restricted to pipeline traffic until 1978, when management of the highway was turned over to the state. Public traffic on the road was allowed only as far as the Yukon River bridge, 56 miles from the Elliott Highway junction. In 1982, the Dalton Highway was opened to public traffic in summer to Disaster Creek at Milepost 211, almost 100 miles north of the Arctic Circle, making it the farthest north public road in the United States. Travel beyond the Disaster Creek checkpoint required a permit from the Alaska Department of Transportation.

The future of public travel on the Dalton Highway was uncertain at press time in early 1983. A major concern since the opening of the first 211 miles of the Dalton to the public was the fragile environment of the pipeline corridor, a 12- to 24-mile-wide strip of land extending some 300 miles from the Elliott Highway to pump station number 2. (The pipeline corridor was under the control of the Bureau of Land Management, but the State of Alaska was attempting to acquire control of it in 1982.)

From its turnoff on the Elliott Highway, the Dalton Highway winds north along the pipeline, paralleling and sometimes crossing the 48-inch-in-diameter pipe. Slightly less

Yukon River bridge at Milepost 56 of the Dalton Highway was the farthest north point for public travel until 1982, when the road was open to public travel north to Milepost 211. The 2,290-foot-long bridge replaced hovercrafts that were used to carry freight across the river. (Sharon Paul, staff)

Left — Sunrise at Pump Station No. 6, Milepost 54 on the Dalton Highway, is at 2:30 A.M. in mid-June. This is one of a dozen pump stations along the 800-mile-long trans-Alaska pipeline that help move oil from the North Slope to Valdez. (Glen Forster)

Right — Wayne Conley, longtime Alaskan and ardent fisherman, with grayling he caught in the Jim River, Milepost 141. (Sharon Paul, staff)

Bears are sometimes seen along the Dalton, and some have learned that humans are a good source of food: a dangerous situation for both bears and humans. It is against the law to feed wildlife. (Sharon Paul, staff)

205

Silvery line across the landscape is the trans-Alaska pipeline. More than half of the 800-mile-long pipeline is above ground because of permafrost conditions; melting permafrost would create difficult soil stability problems. (Sharon Paul, staff)

Don Burt and Kathy Money at their Coldfoot cafe advertised as the "world's farthest north truck stop." Located about 174 miles up the highway, theirs is one of two service stops along the road.
(Sharon Paul, staff)

than half of the 800-mile-long pipeline between Prudhoe Bay and Valdez is buried; the remainder is on above-ground supports. Views along the Dalton take in hundreds of square miles of unpopulated land: scrub spruce, birch, willow, and alder near the Yukon River; wild flowers and low hills farther north; and the treeless tundra of the North Slope. There are few visitor services; gas, food, and rest rooms are available at the Yukon River bridge and at Coldfoot, Milepost 173.6. North of the Disaster Creek checkpoint, the highway enters the Brooks Range, crosses 4,800-foot Atigun Pass, then descends to the North Slope. The northern limit of the state-owned highway is just short of the Prudhoe Bay oil operations.

Gas station at the Yukon River bridge is the first service stop on the Dalton; the next public services are more than 100 miles north of here.
(Sharon Paul, staff)

Remote and beautiful Brooks Range is crossed by the Dalton Highway about 171 miles south of Prudhoe Bay. Travel this far north on the highway requires a permit. (Sharon Paul, staff)

Above — *The Dalton Highway ends a few miles short of Prudhoe Bay and the Arctic Ocean. Travel beyond this point, as the sign says, is by permission of the oil companies.*
(Third Eye Photography)

Right — *Oil company bus at Prudhoe Bay carries workers between dormitories and drill sites.* (Third Eye Photography)

209

Clockwise from right — *The state ferry* Aurora, *shown here docking at Hollis, connects Ketchikan with Prince of Wales Island.* (Rollo Pool, staff)

A drive up Harbor Mountain Road behind Sitka leads to scenic panoramas, such as this view of Starrigavan Bay. (Rollo Pool, staff)

Tongass Highway follows west shore of Revillagigedo Island along Tongass Narrows. South Tongass Highway deadends 13 miles from Ketchikan. (Sharon Paul, staff)

BUSH ROADS

Highways cover only about one-third of Alaska; the rest of the state comes under the heading of "Bush," a vast region of varying geography that is accessible only by air or by water. There are roads in the Bush (though none are connected to the main highway system), ranging from a few miles of gravel road, like Kotzebue's two-mile-long state highway, to more extensive road systems, such as that on Prince of Wales Island. But the bulk of transportation in Alaska's Bush regions is by water craft — ferries, ships, and barges — or by aircraft.

Southeastern Alaska has several local highways, made accessible to vehicles by a state ferry system that moves people and cars from town to town. Ketchikan's Tongass Highway, the 16-mile Zimovia Highway at Wrangell, Petersburg's Mitkof Highway, and local roads at Sitka and other Southeastern towns provide access to airports, campgrounds, fishing spots, and other attractions. Juneau's Glacier Highway connects with the spur road to Mendenhall Glacier and to the Auke Bay ferry terminal. Many of the highways in Southeastern were, and still are, logging roads. Prince of Wales Island has three main gravel roads connecting the communities of Hollis, Klawock, Craig, and Thorne Bay, and miles of logging roads and spurs to other points on the island.

For Southeastern destinations not on the ferry route or local highways, transportation is by airplane or boat. Glacier Bay, one of Southeastern Alaska's major attractions, can be reached only by airplane, cruise ship, or private boat.

The state's Southwestern ferry system provides service to the island of Kodiak and some ports on the Alaska Peninsula. Kodiak also has 87 miles of gravel road covering the northeastern end of the island, most of it built to connect outlying farms with the community of Kodiak. But most travel in Southwestern Alaska is by air. The far-flung Aleutian Islands, a chain stretching 1,400 miles west from the Alaska mainland,

Above — *Floatplane refuels at city float along Ketchikan's waterfront. Small plane travel is a common form of transportation throughout Alaska, and a necessary one in the Bush.* (Sharon Paul, staff)

Below — *All big things come by barge to Yukon River communities. This barge is unloading a truck and supplies at Ruby.* (Betsy Hart)

Left — *Mitkof Highway leads south from Petersburg along Wrangell Narrows, ending 34 miles from town at Sumner Strait. This rocky beach is located at Mile 23 of the highway.* (Rollo Pool, staff)

Below — *Local highways in Southeastern Alaska, such as Wrangell's Zimovia Highway, lead out to quiet coves, shady picnic sites, and campsites.* (Staff)

Loaded logging trucks are a common sight on Prince of Wales Island roads. The heavily forested island is 45 miles west of Ketchikan by ferry. (Rollo Pool, staff)

212

Spur road off Glacier Highway leads to the face of Mendenhall Glacier, 13 miles from downtown Juneau. (Sharon Paul, staff)

Above — Aerial view of the spectacular Fairweather Range east of Yakutat. Much of Alaska's rugged terrain is accessible only by plane. (Rollo Pool, staff)

Left — Juneau's Gastineau Channel, like most Southeastern waterways, is usually busy with plane and ship traffic. (Sharon Paul, staff)

Two views of Kodiak's
Chiniak Road: above, the road
winds down the east side of
Kodiak Island, passing the
airport near the mouth of
Women's Bay; right, Chiniak
Road passes through a
ranching area some
20 miles south of Kodiak. In a
1929 letter to the Alaska Road
Commission, Kodiak's
Chamber of Commerce
petitioned for "suitable
highways" to connect area
homesteads. The island
currently has 87 miles of road.
(Both photos by Sharon Paul, staff)

is served by commercial airliners. Bush aircraft are the lifeline of scattered villages on the Alaska Peninsula and the major means of transportation to Katmai National Park and other attractions on the Alaska Peninsula.

Funds (or lack of them) and the geography of Alaska precluded road building west from Anchorage and Fairbanks across the great Interior to the Bering Sea coast. In the early days of the territory, Alaska's navigable streams — the Yukon, Kuskokwim, Innoko, Koyukuk, Tanana, and other rivers — made natural highways. Road construction was a slow and expensive process, and the Alaska Road Commission did "not spend money upon the construction of summer roads to parallel river routes," as ARC president James G. Steese wrote in April 1924. Alaska's great rivers, like the Yukon, are still used as summer highways in this mostly roadless region, plied by freight-carrying barges, the skiffs of local fishermen, or residents boating downriver to visit friends. In winter, snow machines are used to travel the frozen rivers and land, replacing the dog sleds of earlier days.

Even in the remote region of the Bering Sea coast, the Interior, and the Arctic, roads exist. Most were begun as wagon roads, linking gold mining localities with the head of navigation. On the Seward Peninsula, area roads connect Nome with Teller, Taylor and Council; all were centers of gold mining at

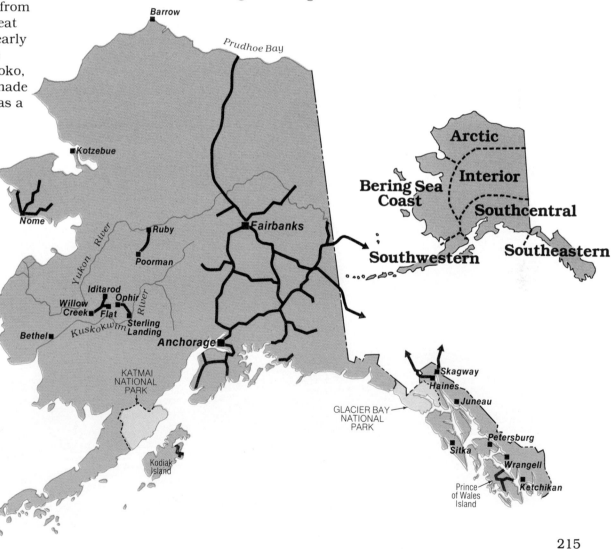

Left — *Kotzebue's Front Street is almost a part of the beach along Kotzebue Sound. This Western Alaska community of more than 2,000 people also has a two-mile-long state highway.* (Penny Rennick, staff)

Below — *Nome, a city of 3,000 on the Bering Sea, is reached by air from Anchorage or Fairbanks. Ocean-going ships and barges bring in supplies for Nome's citizens in the summer. The few highways in the Nome area are rough roads that lead to old gold mining centers.* (Jim Cline)

the turn of the century. In the Interior, the old mining settlement of Poorman is connected by road with Ruby, another old mining settlement located on the important Yukon River. The North Slope Haul Road (Dalton Highway) was built in 1974 to connect the Prudhoe Bay oil field in the Arctic with Fairbanks.

The growth of commercial aviation in the 1930s did away with the need for road building in much of Alaska's Bush. The Territorial Highway Board noted in their 1933-1934 report that "there is no question but that airplanes have diverted much winter travel from the land and it may be that in time no dog sled traveling will be done at all." Today, jet aircraft and Bush planes provide transportation to the most isolated destinations. Nome, some 500 miles west of Anchorage and Fairbanks, is a two-hour plane ride from those cities; Barrow, near the most northern point in the United States (Point Barrow), is an hour and a half by air from Fairbanks. Tour groups from Anchorage fly 800 miles west to the Pribilofs, a rocky group of islands far out in the Bering Sea, to observe fur seals and seabirds.

"A digest of attractions not accessible via the connected highways" has been included in *The MILEPOST®* since the chapter "Off the Trail" premiered in the 1953 edition. The list of attractions has increased over the years with the continued growth of commercial aviation and the development of visitor facilities throughout the state. But of the list, only Mount McKinley has become accessible by connected highway.

Left — *Jacques Hart pilots his parents' riverboat down the Yukon River. The Harts operate Ruby Roadhouse and run river tours.* (Betsy Hart)

Below — *Dogs, people, mail, and supplies travel by small plane in Alaska. A dizzying variety of commercial and private aircraft, on wheels, skis, or floats, serve the Bush.* (Joe Johnson)

THE FUTURE

In the years since World War II, the Alcan Highway (more properly "The Alaska Highway" because Aluminum of Canada has a trademark on "Alcan") has grown from around 2,000 miles of road through the wilderness to over three times that . . . and both Canada and Alaska are still building roads as the hunt for more minerals and more oil and gas continues.

Canadian road building has only been slowed by the sluggish mining economy of this early-eighties period. Strong anti-roads sentiments of environmentalist groups have slowed Alaskan road construction, but in the history of the North, there has ever been the cry for "more roads, more trails" and it is inevitable that the road building will continue.

In Canada construction continues on a project to create an all-seasons loop road from the Hay River-Yellowknife country down to the mouth of the Mackenzie and across the northern mountains to the Klondike Loop and the Alaska Highway via the Dempster.

There were early surveys for more westerly highways from the Cassiar-Dease Lake country behind the Coast Mountains to Atlin to still further shorten the Alaska Highway for Pacific Coast motorists.

There are also surveys in the vaults in Alaska for highways (magnificent scenic routes) up the Stikine and Taku rivers from the Wrangell-Petersburg area and from Juneau to connect with the new Canadian Dease Lake-Atlin route.

It doesn't seem so long ago all that was needed was money to complete the Fairbanks to Nome road by joining the Livengood road on the east to the Teller to Nome road on the west.

And there were surveys and cost projections made of highways connecting Anchorage with Bristol Bay and Anchorage with Nome.

Environmentalists and recent arrivals in the North who came, like so many of us, "to escape the rat race" don't want any more roads. But miners, the real estate hungry, and those who proclaim a need to expand tax bases and to reduce people pressure on scenery and wildlife are likely to combine to cause many new roads to yet be built.

Like it or not, it seems to be the American way. Whenever, our MILEPOST editors will be there.

Keep the speed down . . save tire friction and blowouts . . . and cause fewer "Alcan strawberries" on other folks' windshields! And enjoy.

Robert G. Henning
Publisher

Opposite — *Long straight section of the Seward Highway crosses Rabbit Creek on the outskirts of Anchorage. Marshy ground, high mountains, and severe winters are just a few obstacles facing road builders in Alaska.* (Jon R. Nickles)

Above — *A truck is silhouetted against the setting sun at Akulik Camp on the North Slope.*
(Third Eye Photography)

Alaska Geographic® Back Issues

The North Slope, Vol. 1, No. 1. The charter issue of *ALASKA GEOGRAPHIC®* took a long, hard look at the North Slope and the then-new petroleum development at "the top of the world." *Out of print.*

One Man's Wilderness, Vol. 1, No. 2. The story of a dream shared by many, fulfilled by few: a man goes into the bush, builds a cabin and shares his incredible wilderness experience. Color photos. 116 pages, $9.95

Admiralty . . . Island in Contention, Vol. 1, No. 3. An intimate and multifaceted view of Admiralty: its geological and historical past, its present-day geography, wildlife and sparse human population. Color photos. 78 pages, $5.00

Fisheries of the North Pacific: History, Species, Gear & Processes, Vol. 1, No. 4. The title says it all. This volume is out of print, but the book, from which it was excerpted, is available in a revised, expanded large-format volume. 424 pages. $24.95.

The Alaska-Yukon Wild Flowers Guide, Vol. 2, No. 1. First Northland flower book with both large, color photos and detailed drawings of every species described. Features 160 species, common and scientific names and growing height. Vertical-format book edition now available. 218 pages, $10.95.

Richard Harrington's Yukon, Vol. 2, No. 2. The Canadian province with the colorful past *and* present. *Out of print.*

Prince William Sound, Vol. 2, No. 3. This volume explored the people and resources of the Sound. *Out of print.*

Yakutat: The Turbulent Crescent, Vol. 2, No. 4. History, geography, people — and the impact of the coming of the oil industry. *Out of print.*

Glacier Bay: Old Ice, New Land, Vol. 3, No. 1. The expansive wilderness of Southeastern Alaska's Glacier Bay National Monument (recently proclaimed a national park and preserve) unfolds in crisp text and color photographs. Records the flora and fauna of the area, its natural history, with hike and cruise information, plus a large-scale color map. 132 pages, $9.95

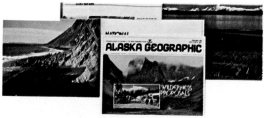

The Land: Eye of the Storm, Vol. 3, No. 2. The future of one of the earth's biggest pieces of real estate! *This volume is out of print,* but the latest on the Alaska lands controversy is detailed completely in Volume 8, Number 4.

Alaska's Volcanoes: Northern Link in the Ring of Fire, Vol. 4, No. 1. Scientific overview supplemented with eyewitness accounts of Alaska's historic volcano eruptions. Includes color and black-and-white photos and a schematic description of the effects of plate movement upon volcanic activity. 88 pages. *Temporarily out of print.*

Wilderness Proposals: Which Way for Alaska's Lands?, Vol. 4, No. 4. This volume gave yet another detailed analysis of the many Alaska lands questions. *Out of print.*

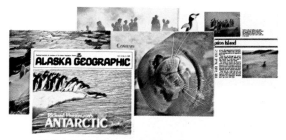

Richard Harrington's Antarctic, Vol. 3, No. 3. The Canadian photojournalist guides readers through remote and little understood regions of the Antarctic and Subantarctic. More than 200 color photos and a large fold-out map. 104 pages, $8.95

The Brooks Range: Environmental Watershed, Vol. 4, No. 2. An impressive work on a truly impressive piece of Alaska — The Brooks Range. *Out of print.*

Cook Inlet Country, Vol. 5, No. 1. A visual tour of the region — its communities, big and small, and its countryside. Begins at the southern tip of the Kenai Peninsula, circles Turnagain Arm and Knik Arm for a close-up view of Anchorage, and visits the Matanuska and Susitna valleys and the wild, west side of the inlet. 230 color photos, separate map. 144 pages, $9.95

The Silver Years of the Alaska Canned Salmon Industry: An Album of Historical Photos, Vol. 3, No. 4. The grand and glorious past of the Alaska canned salmon industry. *Out of print.*

Kodiak: Island of Change, Vol. 4, No. 3. Russians, wildlife, logging and even petroleum . . . an island where change is one of the few constants. *Out of print.*

Southeast: Alaska's Panhandle, Vol. 5, No. 2. Explores Southeastern Alaska's maze of fjords and islands, mossy forests and glacier-draped mountains — from Dixon Entrance to Icy Bay, including all of the state's fabled Inside Passage. Along the way are profiles of every town, together with a look at the region's history, economy, people, attractions and future. Includes large fold-out map and seven area maps. 192 pages, $12.95.

Bristol Bay Basin, Vol. 5, No. 3. Explores the land and the people of the region known to many as the commercial salmon-fishing capital of Alaska. Illustrated with contemporary color and historic black-and-white photos. Includes a large fold-out map of the region. 96 pages, $9.95.

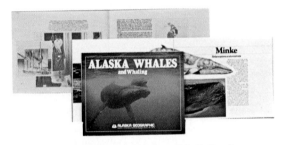

Alaska Whales and Whaling, Vol. 5, No. 4. The wonders of whales in Alaska — their life cycles, travels and travails — are examined, with an authoritative history of commercial and subsistence whaling in the North. Includes a fold-out poster of 14 major whale species in Alaska in perspective, color photos and illustrations, with historical photos and line drawings. 144 pages, $12.95.

Yukon-Kuskokwim Delta, Vol. 6, No. 1. This volume explored the people and lifestyles of one of the most remote areas of the 49th state. *Out of print.*

The Aurora Borealis, Vol. 6, No. 2. Here one of the world's leading experts - Dr. S.-I. Akasofu of the University of Alaska — explains in an easily understood manner, aided by many diagrams and spectacular color and black-and-white photos, what causes the aurora, how it works, how and why scientists are studying it today and its implications for our future. 96 pages, $7.95.

Alaska's Native People, Vol. 6, No. 3. In this edition the editors examine the varied worlds of the Inupiat Eskimo, Yup'ik Eskimo, Athabascan, Aleut, Tlingit, Haida and Tsimshian. Included are sensitive, informative articles by Native writers, plus a large, four-color map detailing the Native villages and defining the language areas. 304 pages, $24.95.

The Stikine, Vol. 6, No 4. River route to three Canadian gold strikes in the 1800s. This edition explores 400 miles of Stikine wilderness, recounts the river's paddlewheel past and looks into the future. Illustrated with contemporary color photos and historic black-and-white; includes a large fold-out map. 96 pages, $9.95.

Alaska's Great Interior, Vol. 7, No. 1. Alaska's rich Interior country, west from the Alaska-Yukon Territory border and including the huge drainage between the Alaska Range and the Brooks Range, is covered thoroughly. Included are the region's people, communities, history, economy, wilderness areas and wildlife. Illustrated with contemporary color and black-and-white photos. Includes a large fold-out map. 128 pages, $9.95.

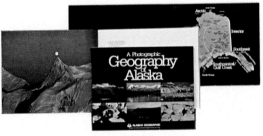

A Photographic Geography of Alaska, Vol. 7, No. 2. An overview of the entire state — a visual tour through the six regions of Alaska: Southeast, Southcentral/Gulf Coast, Alaska Peninsula and Aleutians, Bering Sea Coast, Arctic and Interior. Plus a handy appendix of valuable information — "Facts About Alaska." Approximately 160 color and black-and-white photos and 35 maps. 192 pages, $14.95.

The Aleutians, Vol. 7, No. 3. Home of the Aleut, a tremendous wildlife spectacle, a major World War II battleground and now the heart of a thriving new commercial fishing industry. Contemporary color and black-and-white photographs, and a large fold-out map. 224 pages, $14.95.

Alaska Mammals, Vol. 8, No. 2. From tiny ground squirrels to the powerful polar bear, and from the tundra hare to the magnificent whales inhabiting Alaska's waters, this volume includes 80 species of mammals found in Alaska. Included are beautiful color photographs and personal accounts of wildlife encounters. 184 pages, $12.95.

Alaska's Glaciers, Vol. 9, No. 1. Examines in-depth the massive rivers of ice, their composition, exploration, present-day distribution and scientific significance. Illustrated with many contemporary color and historical black-and-white photos, the text includes separate discussions of more than a dozen glacial regions. 144 pages, $9.95.

Klondike Lost: A Decade of Photographs by Kinsey & Kinsey, Vol. 7, No. 4. An album of rare photographs and all-new text about the lost Klondike boom town of Grand Forks, second in size only to Dawson during the gold rush. Introduction by noted historian Pierre Berton: 138 pages, area maps and more than 100 historical photos, most never before published. $12.95.

The Kotzebue Basin, Vol. 8, No. 3. Examines northwestern Alaska's thriving trading area of Kotzebue Sound and the Kobuk and Noatak river basins. Contemporary color and historical black-and-white photographs. 184 pages, $12.95.

Sitka and Its Ocean/Island World, Vol. 9, No. 2. From the elegant capital of Russian America to a beautiful but modern port, Sitka, on Baranof Island, has become a commercial and cultural center for Southeastern Alaska. Pat Roppel, longtime Southeast resident and expert on the region's history, examines in detail the past and present of Sitka, Baranof Island, and neighboring Chichagof Island. Illustrated with contemporary color and historical black-and-white photographs. 128 pages, $9.95.

Wrangell-Saint Elias, Vol. 8, No. 1. Mountains, including the continent's second- and fourth-highest peaks, dominate this international wilderness that sweeps from the Wrangell Mountains in Alaska to the southern Saint Elias range in Canada. Illustrated with contemporary color and historical black-and-white photographs. Includes a large fold-out map. 144 pages, $9.95.

Alaska National Interest Lands, Vol. 8, No. 4. Following passage of the bill formalizing Alaska's national interest land selections (d-2 lands), longtime Alaskans Celia Hunter and Ginny Wood review each selection, outlining location, size, access, and briefly describing the region's special attractions. Illustrated with contemporary color photographs. 242 pages, $14.95.

Islands of the Seals: The Pribilofs, Vol. 9, No. 3.
Great herds of northern fur seals drew Russians and
Aleuts to these remote Bering Sea islands where they
founded permanent communities and established a
unique international commerce. The communities
languished under U.S. control until recent decades
when new legislation and attempts at economic
diversification have increased interest in the islands,
their Aleut people, and the rich marine resources
nearby. Illustrated with contemporary color and
historical black-and-white photographs. 128 pages,
$9.95.

**Alaska's Oil/Gas & Minerals Industry, Vol. 9,
No. 4.** Experts detail the geological processes and
resulting mineral and fossil fuel resources that are
now in the forefront of Alaska's economy.
Discussions of historical methods and the latest
techniques in present-day mining, submarine
deposits, taxes, regulations, and education
complete this overview of an important state
industry. Illustrated with historical black-and-
white and contemporary color photographs. 216
pages, $12.95.

The Alaska Geographic Society

Box 4-EEE, Anchorage, AK 99509

Membership in The Alaska Geographic Society is
$30, which includes the following year's four
quarterlies which explore a wide variety of subjects in
the Northland, each issue an adventure in great
photos, maps, and excellent research. Members
receive their quarterlies as part of the membership fee
at considerable savings over the prices which
nonmembers must pay for the following book
editions.